Godly

Leadership

David Teague
with Harvey Shepard

ALMOND TREE
PUBLICATIONS

ALMOND TREE PUBLICATIONS
This book is also being published in a separate edition by
Interserve International
as a part of their "Grassroots Missions Series."

GODLY LEADERSHIP

ISBN   1451596723
EAN-13   9781451596724

Contents

Introduction
What the World Yearns For

Leaders are everywhere. They include not just the politicians and executives of this world, but any person who makes things happen. A typical mid-sized hospital, for instance, will have over 100 leaders — including all the nurses, physicians and staff who lead the teams that allow a hospital to function.

A leader is anyone who influences others toward a goal. We lead by initiating, organizing, managing, envisioning, guiding, nurturing and mentoring — to name a few of the ways of leading. We may be given an official title, or just rise to leadership in a single situation. Even in a family, we are leaders simply by being parents. In some traditions, a couple is crowned when they are married to symbolize their leadership roles in the world as husband and wife.

Leaders are everywhere, but what is lacking in many leaders is spiritual depth.

Distrust in leadership is an ever-recurrent theme in the news. As I write, an American governor who seriously lied refuses to resign. In Europe, a prime minister is suspected of releasing a terrorist for oil contracts. And in China, a major business scandal has erupted involving an important mining company. Every day carries similar news stories about compromised leadership.

Closer to home, we all have our stories of leaders who have disappointed us. It could be a pastor who shattered the trust of a church. Or a colleague who sabotaged a project. We may even be questioning our own role in some difficult situation.

One thing is certain: we are tired of the shallowness. We want our leaders to be deep people — men and women whom we can respect and trust. This book is for all Christians who want to be like that by deepening their spiritual lives until their leadership reflects God's character.

Originally, this book was developed for the partners of Interserve, an international Christian service organization. However, it is also designed for all leaders in every situation: team and project leaders in organizations, executives and managers in business, as well as pastors and lay leaders in churches.

The intent of *Godly Leadership* is to help leaders become spiritually-formed. Many books about spiritual formation seem ethereal and irrelevant to the steely world of leaders. And most books about leadership totally ignore spirituality, as if leaders lack souls. Our goal is to distill the best thinking about spiritual formation and present it in a way that is relevant to leaders.

To do this, we need a framework for our thoughts. Henri Nouwen (1932-1996), the influential theologian of spirituality, provides one. He noticed a three-fold pattern in Jesus' own leadership. First, he said, Jesus communed with his Father. Then, Jesus built a community with his apostles. Lastly, Jesus ministered to people.

In our book, we have adopted and adapted Nouwen. We suggest that we become godly leaders by becoming authentic with God and then authentic with people. Then, out of this pool of authenticity, our spirituality naturally begins to influence how we lead. Following this plan, the three main parts of this book are:

Becoming Authentic with God

Becoming Authentic with People

Becoming Spiritual in Leadership

I wish to thank Dr. Harvey Shepard who has kindly agreed to enhance this book by contributing Chapter Ten, "Picturing Community." It is based on his master's thesis on Christian community and is a most valuable addition.

David P. Teague

PART ONE
Becoming Authentic with God

1

Leaders Who Are Spiritual

What makes people to be good leaders? We have been wondering about that question since the dawn of time, but only since the beginning of the 20th century have we sought to answer it in a scientific way. So, what have we been learning?

One of the things we have been discovering is that spirituality plays an important role in leadership. While we cannot explore all the vast research about leadership since 1900, we can trace the growing awareness of the significance of spirituality.

Beginning around 1900, the earliest research on leadership sought to isolate the **personality traits** of good leaders. It was thought that once these traits were identified, then anyone who aspires to be a leader could emulate them to achieve success.

This early research into personality traits ended in failure. It was discovered that leaders have widely varying traits, so no definitive list of traits could be produced. Furthermore, merely imitating a leader proved to be no guarantee of success. Mimicry is not the same as personal authenticity.

After the failure of this early research, the emphasis in the middle of the 20th century shifted away from investigating traits to studying **behaviors.** Researchers sought to answer the question, "What behaviors produce the best results?" It was discovered that leaders are more effective when they care about people and not just about goals since their team members will be more loyal and satisfied.

Further work explored the **relationship** between leader and follower. James M. Burns' book *Leadership* (1978) popularized the concept of the "transformational" leader — someone who inspires followers to transcend their own self-interests for the good of the group. In contrast, "transactional" leaders focus most of their energy on such things as enforcing rules, regulations and requirements.

Another seminal book was Robert K. Greenleaf's *Servant Leadership* (1977). Before Greenleaf, we understood leadership as leaders and followers. In contrast, Greenleaf saw leadership as flowing out of who we are as authentic people in relationship with others. Greenleaf's thinking led to the development of the leader-team model in which a leader is conceived as a "first among equals."

Because of Greenleaf's focus on relationships and personal genuineness, it was natural for leadership studies to begin thinking about the interior life of a leader. By the mid-1990's, researchers began studying the *spirituality* of leaders. Leadership researchers use the phrase "spiritual leadership" to refer to a leader's inner integrity and authenticity.

Utilizing sociological research, studies quickly produced interesting results. In particular, they vindicated such traditional spiritual virtues as integrity, honesty and humility. A 2005 cross study of 150 reports by Laura Reave concluded:

> All of the following practices have ... been found to be crucial leadership skills: showing respect for others, demonstrating fair treatment, expressing caring and concern, listening responsively, recognizing the contributions of others, and engaging in reflective practice.

Her findings also refute the Machiavellian leader:

> Many experts expect strategy, intelligence, even ruthlessness to be marks of a successful leader ... Instead, spiritual values such as integrity, honesty, and humility have been repeatedly found to be key elements of leadership success. [1]

---

[1]   Laura Reave, "Spiritual Values and Practices Related to Leadership Effectiveness" in The Leadership Quarterly (Volume 16, Issue 5, October 2005, Pages 655-687).

As we look back over these leadership studies, there has been a gradual shift from just identifying external traits and behaviors of a leader to understanding the crucial role that personal authenticity plays in leadership. Increasingly, we have been learning of the importance of spirituality in making good leaders.

To be godly leaders, however, we have to do more than just say, "I'll try to be more authentic now." We become authentic by meeting God in our hearts and by developing deep relationships with others. Those are the subjects we'll be exploring in the chapters ahead.

2
Human Brokenness

The brokenness of our lives is the growing edge of our faith. This is perhaps the most fundamental principle behind spiritual formation, and possibly the most misunderstood.

It tells us that true spiritual growth happens only when we struggle with the deepest, darkest parts of our lives and experience God there.

Many fail to grow spiritually because they approach the subject rationally. We feel that if we just try hard enough, we can do whatever we want. This is a by-product of the modernist era, which held that the mind holds absolute control over the body. But people who think they can become perfect in their own strength do not understand grace.

OUR IRRATIONAL SIDE
We are more irrational than we may realize. In one famous experiment in the 1970's, Dr. Benjamin Libet found that our brains signal us to perform an action a fraction of a second *before* we consciously

"choose" to do the action. This suggests that the irrational, subconscious part of our minds controls us far more than we recognize.

The Apostle Paul acknowledged this irrational side of our minds in words that recall a dog chasing its own tail:

> I do not understand what I do. For what I want to do I do not do, but what I hate I do ... What I do is not the good I want to do; no, the evil I do not want to do − this I keep on doing. (Romans 7:15, 19)

Since the time of the psychiatrist Carl Jung (1875-1961), some have given a sinister label to this irrationality — calling it the "shadow side" or the "dark side." Such labels simply are meant to describe all the suppressed emotions, unresolved fears, urges and conflicts that linger within our psyches.

The shadow side is the repository for our human brokenness. All our sorrows and unsettled pain from the traumas of life collect there, including all our unresolved grief, our failures and all the abandonments we have experienced. The shadow side also easily partners with what the Bible calls our sinful nature.

Our shadow side resembles the moray eel that lurks in an ocean crevice — all may seem calm and serene until the moment when the eel suddenly lunges and strikes. We may think we are completely in control until the day comes when we find ourselves doing some stupid, self-destructive thing.

For instance, psychological researchers have found a high correlation between a "strict, repressive religious upbringing" and sex offenses. This does not mean that people from caring, Christian homes are going to turn into dangerous sex criminals. The emphasis is on repression, not on being Christian. What it does imply is that a reliance on rules alone, no matter how strictly enforced, is inadequate in suppressing the shadow side.

I once knew a thoracic surgeon, a brilliant man, who treated the cancer victims of smoking. He smoked himself to death — dying of the same, painful disease he sought to cure in others. At his funeral, his best friend from their medical school days spoke of the incredible mind this man had. But then he said, incredulously, "Why did he do it? Why did he smoke? He knew better. It was so irrational."

A great deal of human behavior arises from our irrational side — from our instincts, impulses, habits, reactions and raw emotions. Some even say that only 5% (if that much!) of human behavior is rational and planned. This is true even for Christians who were, on last check, still human.

Just this last week I spoke to an earnest Christian man who had begun to binge drink. It's just a symptom of the deeper problems in his life of chronic unemployment and depression. It's true that he is a believer, but in his hopelessness, his irrational side is beginning to engulf him.

We all suffer from irrationality to some degree. We hardly want to admit it and, in truth, we usually cannot fully acknowledge our own dysfunctions. Yet, our irrational side can make us:

- fall into an addiction like pornography
- become overly controlling
- think that we are superior to others
- be unable to form deep, lasting relationships
- feel distrustful or always anxious
- be overly sensitive to criticism
- be unable to walk away from harmful situations

Irrationality also affects the groups to which we belong. Here is a list of some of the most common indicators of dysfunction in families and groups. Have any of them been present in your family or within the teams you have led?

- issues are not openly discussed
- people are not allowed to express themselves
- there is lying ... information is withheld
- communication happens through third-parties
- there is denial
- conflict is accepted as normal

- there is a lack of empathy
- people do not feel safe around each other
- love is conditional
- rules are vague or inconsistent
- personal boundaries are not respected
- people are unable to adapt
- people always expect perfection

THE ROLE AND SOUL OF A LEADER

Leaders are like actors who play a role. People expect us to be wise, encouraging and visionary and, to the best of our abilities, we try to live up to these expectations. We try to present ourselves rationally.

In reality, though, the public personas we project on stage are quite different from our private lives. As leaders we often feel the disconnect between what we do and who we really are. Alone, we might find ourselves feeling confused and discouraged, or struggling with self-doubt and resentment. The soul-numbing pressures and demands of our jobs can cause us to grow out-of-touch with ourselves.

Added to this is the inherent capacity at self-deception which we are all born with and which just gets worse when we lead — a deception that deludes us into thinking that all is well, even while our souls wither inside us.

We cannot hide from the irrational in us. It dogs us through life and affects how we lead. We all have seen leaders who are not soul-healthy. Just think about the worst boss you ever had! Perhaps it was a person who always had to be in control. Or always had to please everyone. Or was unusually angry, suspicious or jealous.

Sometimes we have time-bombs ticking away deep within us: perhaps we grew up in an alcoholic or an abusive home and have unresolved issues that threaten to explode without notice. This can lead to risky decisions and a breakdown in relationships that impairs our ability to get things done as leaders.

Some leaders have a subtle tendency to make everything revolve around them so they can look good. Without knowing it, they're narcissists. Wayne Hochwarter, a management professor at Florida State University College of Business, surveyed more than 1,200 employees. He found that 31% percent of the employees reported having a narcissistic boss who exaggerated his or her accomplishments. Hockwarter also found that these leaders created a toxic environment around whom "the team perspective ceases to exist, and the work environment becomes increasingly stressful." Often, such leaders are unaware of how others perceive them.

Power is another point of deception for leaders. In another research study done through the

Kellogg School of Management at Northwestern University, when people were given power, they tended to be stricter in how they judged others and more lenient toward their own shortcomings. In other words, the study found that power tends to turn us into moral hypocrites.

Playing the role of leader can also distort our sense of self-identity. If we start basing our self-identity on our position or title, then we will feel innately more significant than others, when we really are not.

As leaders, we may be totally unaware of our own time-bombs, narcissism, moral hypocrisy or distorted self-identity. Since we are so good at hiding our vulnerabilities and weaknesses, we may be unable to discern the state of our souls. Deficiencies that are glaringly plain to others may go completely unnoticed by us.

To serve well, though, we must be well. To avoid any disconnect between role and soul in our lives, we need to find a way to nourish our hearts. When we are healthy within, we will move from merely playing a role as a leader to exercising true, authentic leadership.

THE GOOD SIDE OF THE SHADOW SIDE

Our human brokenness is not all gloom and doom, but also has a good side. The deepest pain we feel from our fears and disappointments can also become the motivation that fuels our strongest drives.

Doris Kearns Goodwin wrote about Lyndon Johnson, the American president of the 1960's. Early in life, Johnson lost the hand of a young woman when her father rejected Johnson as "not good enough." This rejection created a burning desire within Johnson to prove his worth. When he arrived in Washington D.C. as a senator in the 1950's, he worked relentlessly until he achieved the center of senatorial power.

Goodwin writes about Johnson's shadow side — how he was deeply manipulative because he always felt a need to be loved and in control. However, Johnson's driven, manipulative personality perfectly matched the backroom politics of the Senate. It turned him into one of the most effective senators ever, especially when he passed major civil rights legislation in that still-prejudiced country.

Our shadow side is intrinsic to us. Just as we cannot outrun our own shadow on a sunny day, none of us can deny who we are. To do so would be to disown our own humanity. We are who we are, and God knows this. He understands our humanity and had a hand in shaping our personalities. God does not want us to be false to ourselves. Instead, he desires us to be honest about our humanity so we can experience his transforming grace.

As one international leader, Bob Morris, wrote to me:

> So often we see our basic personality as a problem, but how can a leopard change its spots? As I reflected on this, I thought of temper being transformed into righteous indignation, stubbornness into perseverance, and an inferiority complex becoming a servant heart. This gives us hope for God's transforming grace — not to change our personalities as much as sanctifying what we are.

When we have a healthy soul, we become authentic leaders. The first step to this authenticity is to recognize the existence of our own human brokenness within. When we realize that we are no longer in control, we become freer to grow spiritually. In the next chapter, we will see how we can bring our brokenness to God.

3
Coming Alive

The heart is the place where we come to know God. Whenever we are honest about ourselves in our hearts to him, we have made an appointment for a meeting.

The heart is not simply our emotional nature, as we may think, but the core of our being. It is the motivational hub out of which spring all our values and actions, emotions, intellect, habits and will. Proverbs 4:23 advises us, "Above all else, guard your heart for it is the wellspring of life."

If we wish to become authentic in our relationship with God, we have to know our hearts. But Jeremiah once said, "The heart is deceitful above all things and beyond cure. Who can understand it?" (Jeremiah 17:9). If we are all prone to self-deception, how can we possibly know ourselves and God?

The ancient Greeks taught that we can know our hearts by enduring a trial. So, Greek mythology speaks of the twelve trials of Hercules and of Odysseus' twenty-year trek home from Troy.

Today, many leaders use endurance courses to test themselves. Such training may help us to know more about our limits, but something more is needed to know God than just acting like a modern Hercules in a wilderness course . . .

Through the ages, others have taught that we know our hearts by enduring temptation — especially that of power. Abraham Lincoln, the 16th president of the United States, once said, "Nearly all men can stand adversity, but if you want to test a man's character, give him power." Having power, we are forced to think about our values. Will we use our power for personal gain or to manipulate people? The temptation of power reveals much about our character. But still, we need something else to know God . . .

Many people gain self-knowledge through therapy sessions and group meetings. Once again, these can be helpful ways to navigate the labyrinths of self-deception within our own hearts. They can teach us about ourselves, but still we need something more . . .

There is yet one more path to knowing ourselves, the truest of all. St. Augustine (354-430 AD) shows it to us in his autobiography, known to us as his *Confessions*.

In one famous passage, he obsesses over the day he stole some pears as a boy. This hardly seems to be material for a tell-all confession, yet in his *Confessions*, Augustine is telling us the story of his soul. On the day he took those pears, he lost his innocence. He was Adam in the Garden again, snitching God's forbidden fruit and deceiving himself in the grabbing. It was the first of many drubbings he gave his soul, leading into years of self-deception and self-absorption.

Augustine also writes of the day, years later, when he came to know God. He had become convinced of the Gospel by then, but he could not free himself from his lusts. In agony, he went into a garden to wrestle with his soul. There, with tears flowing profusely down his face, Augustine hears a child in a neighboring house call out the words, "*Tolle, lege*" — "Pick it up! Read it!" Thinking it to be a sign from God, Augustine picks up the copy of Romans he has with him and his eyes randomly fall on the words:

> ... not in orgies and drunkenness, not in sexual immorality and debauchery, not in dissension and jealousy. Rather, clothe yourselves with the Lord Jesus Christ, and do not think about how to gratify the desires of the sinful nature. (Romans 13:13-14)

"As the sentence ended," Augustine writes, "there was infused in my heart something like the light of full certainty and all the gloom of doubt vanished away. [1]

He was free. Later, he was to write, "To hear from You about oneself is to know oneself."[2]

Augustine's story tells us that all attempts at self-knowledge are inadequate compared to an encounter with the living God. Only God's searing presence and enabling grace can show us what we truly are and also free us at the same time. When we come to this moment of realization, it is often marked with tears and shame, yet also with release and joy, as we realize that Christ really did die for us. St. Isaiah the Solitary, one of the early desert fathers, said:

> We do not see our sins unless we sever ourselves from them with a feeling of revulsion. Those who have reached this level pray to God with tears, and are filled with shame when they recall their evil love of the passions. [3]

Tears are truth. The Psalmist versifies about tearless, unrepentant people who "flatter themselves too much to detect or hate their sin"

---

1   Augustine, Confessions 8.12

2   Confessions 10.3

3   On Guarding the Intellect, 17

(Psalm 36:1-2). But when we encounter the living God, we know we cannot play games anymore. He is too much the sly detective. When God shines his light upon us, we can no longer hide behind our pride; we can only admit who we are. By so doing, we come to know both God and ourselves.

THE MAKEOVER

God's purpose is our makeover, since salvation is wholeness — eternal and spiritual. The makeover of a human heart takes years since it is heart work, not just head work. We can memorize every verse in the Bible and read every book there is on spiritual formation and still not know what it all means. But when the heart work is done in a genuine way, the result is a growing trust in God's adequacy for us.

The makeover is a process of re-creation: God confronting our selfish and judging spirit, draining the acid out of our hate and converting our stubborn resentment into forgiveness. Spiritual transformation is God descending into the hidden depths of our underground mine, shining his light along the long-darkened path and chiseling out our self-deception.

We may, for instance, know that we belong to Christ yet still habitually lash out at people who criticize us. Then, one day the thought dawns on us, "If Christ is my righteousness, why am I so upset when people criticize me? What does it matter what others think about me? I am living for Christ now, not for myself." Realizing this, we relax. We ease ourselves into God's adequacy. It is the Spirit at work, transforming us, the makeover happening.

The ultimate goal of spiritual formation is always an increasing trust in God's sufficiency for our lives. Without God, we are like people who have to live out of a suitcase — with all the insecurities, fears and wants of being homeless. But when we live with God, we know we have a home. He provides us with security, reassurance and comfort — all the blessings which gradually change us as people.

A LIFE OF CONFESSION

In the years I grew strawberries for my children, my patch produced buckets of spring-sweet berries. However, when I got busy and neglected the patch, it yielded arm-loads of weeds instead.

The human heart is very much like that. Unless we take care, the heart will always revert back to its native species — all the worries, infatuations and frenzies that so easily plague us. Affections for God are a cultivated fruit; they do not come naturally. We need to continually weed our hearts.

Confession is spiritual weeding. It is bending over, taking a close look at our lives and pulling out what needs to go. Confession is when we make our hearts true to God. Done right, confession is good for the soul. It is another way we learn to trust in God's sufficiency.

Again, Augustine teaches us.

His *Confessions* were the world's first autobiography, the most personal literature written until his time. No one had ever read anything like it, especially since they lived in an "honor and shame" world in which no fault was ever admitted.

Never mind, Augustine wrote freely about his faults. About his soul. About his soul struggling to know God. No one ever made themselves look so vulnerable like that on paper before — no one except Augustine. That's why his book proved so powerful, because it knifed through all the Roman hypocrisy of his time. And that's why Augustine so singularly has taught the world what it means to live a life of confession.

He writes:

> The house of my soul is too small for you to come to it. Enlarge it. It is in ruins. Restore it. In your eyes, it looks offensive. I admit it. I know it. But who will clean it up? To whom shall I call other than you? [4]

---

4 Confessions, 1.5

His soul is talking, talking with God. All the time, talking. His soul is seeking, always seeking. Augustine is taking care of his garden. He is paying attention to the state of his heart. But it is not all examination and sorrowful repentance, but a coming alive to God, and then having God transform him and heal him on the inside. Spiritual formation only happens when we are honest to God.

Augustine was perhaps the most important Christian leader in his day. He was such because he took the time to cultivate his heart.

Jesus taught that everything flows out of what we are as people. He once described a heart gone bad: "For out of the heart come evil thoughts, murder, adultery, sexual immorality, theft, false testimony, slander. These are what make a person 'unclean'" (Matthew 15:19-20a). On the other hand, "The good person brings good things out of the good stored up within the heart" (Luke 6:45).

This means, given sufficient time, what is in our hearts will affect the organizations we lead. Narrow leaders will engender narrow organizations. Joyful and expansive leaders will attract people of like spirit and create open, flourishing organizations. Leadership involves more than what we say or do. It flows out of who we are as people.

4
Prayer

What is prayer? Secular people often say that it is no more than a delusion or a sanctified soliloquy in which we address God but really are just talking to ourselves.

Others treat prayer as a form of magic: an attempt to influence events through uttering special words. Such people might refer to prayer as "collective well-wishing" or a "projection of personal power."

Some regard prayer as a recitation. At an earlier point in their lives, they were taught certain prayers. When they pray, they "say" these prayers in fulfillment of what they consider to be a duty to God.

Still others see prayer as a "talk with God." They adopt a casual, conversational approach to God.

Prayer is assuredly not a soliloquy, and it certainly is not magic. But yet, it also seems to be something richer than a dutiful recitation or a casual conversation.

At its heart, *prayer is our relating to God*. When we come alive to God, we start to pray. All of our living to God is a form of prayer. It includes all the ways we interaction with God in our covenant walk. This seems to be the truest and simplest way to understand prayer.

VARIETIES OF PRAYER

Prayer takes on different forms at different times depending on what is happening in our relationship with God. There are as many varieties of prayer as there are ways we relate to God.

When we sense that our sinfulness separates us from God, we naturally begin saying prayers of **confession**. We pray like this because our relationship with God demands it. We know we cannot go on with God until we make things right. A prayer of confession could be as simple as accepting that Jesus died for our sins, or pleading for God to restore our covenant walk.

We also will have times when we become full of gratitude to God. On such occasions, our prayer naturally takes on the form of **giving thanks** and **worship** —telling God who he is, what he has done and what he means to us.

And there will be times when our needs will preoccupy us. Jesus gave us permission to ask God about our basic needs when he taught us to pray for our daily bread. When we look to God to provide for our daily needs, our prayer is a **petition**.

Intercession is pleading with God for others. God especially wants us, as children of the covenant, to pray in a burdened way for others to know him.

All these forms of prayer are verbal. However, since prayer is actually our relating to God, and not just talking to God, this helps us to understand how prayer can be non-verbal as well.

For instance, when we quiet our hearts and minds and tune into God, that is **centering prayer**.

Fasting is a spiritual discipline of weakness by which we remember our utter dependence on God in an effort to be heard by God while praying.

And **abiding prayer** is when we adopt a listening attitude of watching and waiting. It could be as simple as being silent as we seek wisdom or guidance, or asking God a question and waiting for an answer — like the prophet Habakkuk did. This has been called listening prayer, but it is better described as abiding prayer, as will be explained in the next chapter.

Another non-verbal form of prayer is **contemplation**, which is quietly pondering who God is. This is David's gazing upon the "beauty of the Lord" (Psalm 27:4). When we do so, we do not have to use words. We just are enjoying God.

There is also **lived prayer**. It is when our lives are a labor of love to God. St. Benedict (480 – 547) said: "*Laborare est orare*," to labor is to pray. He regarded his work to be a prayer no different than his spoken prayers since he was living his whole life in response to God. In this way, when we do our leadership as an act of love for God, it is a form of prayer. All the meetings, all the headaches in leadership — it is prayer if we do it before God. To lead is to pray.

WORKPLACE SPIRITUALITY

Often, leaders feel frustrated over being "too busy to pray." Indeed, if our work affects our relationship with God, we may be. But if our hearts are right with God, our work itself can be a prayer. This is the central idea behind workplace spirituality.

In Luke 10:38-42, we find the story of Mary and Martha. Since at least the time of Eusebius (c. 263 – c. 339), this story has been misinterpreted to demean workplace spirituality. Mary, who listened quietly to Jesus did the right thing, while Martha's infernal kitchen work made her unspiritual, or so it is said. In the story, however, Jesus did not imply that prayer was superior to work; rather, he was pointing out the needy state of Martha's heart. He did not tell Martha, "Get out of the kitchen!" Rather, he encouraged her to focus on God. She had become too obsessed with the meal.

There is a telling story about workplace spirituality from the life of St. Antony (c. 293-373 AD), the managing founder of monasticism. One day, God reveal to him that someone was more holy than he. The Spirit then led Antony to a woman doing her household chores. She was that person. The point of the story? Workplace spirituality can be as pleasing to God as contemplative spirituality.

In 1520, the Protestant reformer Martin Luther (1483 – 1546) wrote: "The works of monks and priests ... do not differ in the least in the sight of God from the works of the country laborer in the field or a woman going about her household tasks." All work done to love God is equal. The person who prays for a living is not superior to the person who works for a living — if both love God.

Action-orientated leaders need a spirituality that works for them. We find it, not by worrying about the quantity of our prayers but by focusing on our relationship to God. When we approach our spirituality like this, we will seek out times of contemplation to renew our relationship with God, and yet we will also feel confident to work in a bold and hard manner out of sheer love for God.

5
Abiding Prayer

In I Kings 19, the prophet Elijah wanders deep into the desert. His leadership had been a series of dramatic power encounters with the followers of Baal but now he is alone and discouraged. Elijah desperately needs renewal and direction.

Huddled in his mountain cave, Elijah watches as a parade of wind, earthquake and fire go by. His previous ministry had been a drama like that. Fire had fallen from the sky at Mount Carmel. And Elijah had run with supernatural strength through a blinding, wind-driven rain. As a prophet, he really had shaken things up with those followers of Baal.

Now, God is weaning him from all that. The parade over, Elijah encounters a "still, small voice." More precisely, the phrase is the "sound of utter silence." It is God moving in quiet truth within Elijah's heart. On the mountain, God renews Elijah and redirects his ministry.

What happened to Elijah on that mountain can happen to us in our leadership as well. God can speak to our inmost depths and renew our hearts within.

When we come to know God, there is a new life that comes to us. It is the Life Within. Since the place where God meets us is our hearts, we should expect to find his presence there. Jesus said of the Spirit of God, "He lives with you and will be in you" (John 14:17). Indeed, the scriptures speak of the Spirit convicting and instructing our hearts. Paul writes how God's Spirit comforted and encouraged him and even expressed tenderness for him in his heart (Philippians 2:1).

This Life Within is our eternal life, which we have already begun to enjoy. John 15 describes it as the quiet yet steady flow of a life-giving sap within a vine — Christ, who reconciled us to God, being the vine. Remaining in him, we experience the flow of God's eternal life within.

Our attachment to Christ is not a mere connection, but an abiding. This word *abide* is an older English word rich in connotation, suggesting being, dwelling, waiting and resting all at the same time. It is used in our more venerable English translations to describe our relationship to Christ as the Vine as well as our obedience to Christ's commands, especially his command to love one another (John 15:9-17).

It is within this context that we can understand what has been called "listening prayer." It really is *abiding* prayer: having an attitude of attentive listening to God as we abide in Christ.

The phrase "listening prayer" is misleading. When many people first learn about listening prayer, they become excited. "Do you mean to say that God actually speaks to us and we can hear him?" Yes, that's true. But no, there is more to it than that. Many who try listening prayer quickly become discouraged. A common comment is, "I listened to God for an hour and expected to hear something, but I heard nothing. Is something wrong with me?"

No, nothing is wrong, so long as you realize that our goal is not to hear something — it is to be with Someone. That's why "listening prayer" is a misleading title. It creates in people's minds the expectation that they have to hear "words" from God when really all we are expected to do is to abide in Christ.

Thinking of abiding prayer, the famous line from the English poet John Milton comes to mind when he wrote about his blindness: "They also serve who only stand and wait." He saw himself as abiding in the presence of one whose "state is kingly." Even if he did not receive a word from his king, he knows he is still serving in his presence. When we practice abiding prayer, we "stand and wait." We are not trying to hear a word so much as simply to be with God. He may speak, but it comes at his pleasure.

THE VOICE OF GOD

I remember being in a group that was trying to listen for a word from God. We were instructed: "Now it's time to be quiet and listen to God's word for you." Everyone quieted down and tuned their hearts to God.

Just before the exercise began, however, I spotted a pile of candy in the center of the table. So, while people were dutifully waiting for their words from God, I was making little rustling noises as I tried to open a wrapper. The leader cast a pious glare at me and said, "This is listening time now! We need to let God speak!"

As if God could not speak above the rustling of a wrapper . . .

I once lived next to a lion. He was confined in a zoo not far from my apartment in Cairo. I was unable to make him roar. That happened in his own time, usually early in the morning, when things were still. Then, his roar would bellow over the trees and buildings. It would slice right through my closed window and awaken me in my bed where I lay, a kilometer away.

In Jeremiah 23:29, God informs us: "Is not my word like fire and like a hammer that breaks a rock in pieces?" God cannot be forced to speak, but when he does, his voice penetrates like a lion's.

Through the ages, believers have talked about their encounter with the Voice. Several elements always seem to re-occur in the writings. There is talk about the uniqueness of the Voice and how it announces God to us, exalts Jesus, works against Satan and strengthens us in truth and love. The Voice is also a clear and authoritative encounter with God.

This can be distilled into the following:

THE VOICE OF GOD:
- is consistent with the Story of God
- is an encounter with God
- is a call to obey God
- causes us to grow spiritually when we respond

This suggests that what some people call the "voice of God" might be just their own self-talk. We might not want to admit this as a possibility, but when we think that God cannot speak above the rustle of a candy wrapper, or that we can get words from God on cue, perhaps we should at least entertain the idea. After all, it is easy to manufacture a "word" about what we think God is saying to us.

Jeremiah wrote, "Everyone's own word becomes their oracle and so you distort the words of the living God" (Jeremiah 23:36).

How are we, then, to understand the voice of God?

It is a real aspect of our abiding in Christ. As we experience the Life Within as believers, we should expect God to speak to our hearts, but it comes as a gift, not in answer to a demand. More importantly, we cannot listen for God's Voice unless we also practice spiritual discernment, which teaches us the difference between the various voices our souls may hear, namely those of Satan, the self and the Spirit of God.

Because so few people know how to practice spiritual discernment, Protestant, Catholic and Orthodox theologians all have warned through the centuries that private words are the *least* authoritative way of understanding the mind of God. Today, the opposite seems to hold true and private "words" are readily accepted as *more* authoritative by people who seem to know little about discernment.

Yet, unless we practice spiritual discernment, private words can lead to tragic consequences. We all know people who claimed to have a word from the Lord which turned out to be a foolish delusion. The Apostle clearly warns us to "test prophecies" (1 Thessalonians 5:20-21) and to "weigh carefully what is said" (1 Corinthians 14:29). He says we can easily become puffed "up with idle notions"

(Colossians 2:18). The desert fathers and mothers were extremely cautious about mental images that came to monks and they actively warned novices *not* to pay attention to such images, even if they seemed of divine origin.

Given the lack of spiritual discernment among people, the church also has stressed that the *primary* way God speaks to us is through the scriptures and the combined testimony and experience of the community of faith. We may hear God individually, but for us to hear God properly, we must know how to practice spiritual discernment.

This is best done in the context of abiding in Christ with all this means. Abiding in Christ involves sharing in the Body of Christ where we can seek the counsel of others. There is a humility that comes by being in community with God's people, where we experience Christ's reign together. We are best able to discern the true voice of God when we live in humility in Christian community.

Abiding in Christ also involves sharing in the rich tradition of the scriptures, which teach us what God is like — that he is compassionate and gracious, slow to anger and abounding in love and faithfulness, forgiving yet also exacting (Exodus 34:6-7). God's character is also distinctly redemptive (Luke 6:27-36). So, if we hear a "voice" that is cruel or demanding, or lacks grace, we will know immediately that it is not from God and should be rejected.

Abiding in Christ also means that we are to be people of truth. Truth telling is essential to spiritual discernment since Satan is the father of lies. God's Voice does not have to come to us as a lion's roar. It can arrive as still as a whisper, but always it comes in uttermost truth. If we harbor any deceit, we simply cannot hear it.

When we abide in Christ, we certainly should expect to experience the Life Within. There will be times when the Spirit prompts us, warns us, places burdens on our hearts, or speaks a word to the depths of our souls. But we also need to practice spiritual discernment so we can be reasonably certain that when we hear the still, small voice, we will do so in a safe and sure way.

6
Contemplative Prayer

Save Psalm 27 for your next leadership crisis. It's written by a leader who has seen the worst. Opening on a note of confidence, David asserts: "The Lord is my light and my salvation — whom shall I fear?" But then his confidence begins to sound like a whistling among wolves. Verse two casually mentions the gang outside waiting to slit his throat. And, oh yes, the army hunting him down. "No problem," says David. "Even then I will be confident" (vs. 3).

Here is where we begin to mentally wander. Is this man ever going to be real about his fears?

In another psalm, David seems more like the rest of us in our leadership crises: "The enemy pursues me ... my heart within me is dismayed," he says in Psalm 143:3-4. We can relate to such honesty, but Psalm 27 seems like just plain bravissimo.

Actually, it isn't. In Psalm 27 we see David *after* his faith has conquered his fear. We are spared the brutal struggle in his soul so apparent in his other crises. He is showing us his trophy, not the fight.

And David also wants us to know what made the difference for him — gazing upon God:

> One thing I ask of the LORD, that I may dwell in the house of the LORD all the days of my life, to gaze upon the beauty of the LORD and to seek him in his temple. For in the day of trouble he will keep me safe in his dwelling. (Psalm 27:4-5)

This gazing upon the beauty of the Lord is not an idle twittering of time for David. It is what kept him sane when his emotions were running wild as a leader. In a perfect storm, he had found a perfect shelter.

We call this gazing upon God, *contemplation*. It's a form of prayer, the kind in which we do not talk to God so much as we enjoy God for who he is.

Contemplation begins with meditation — filling our minds with who God is in the biblical revelation. We remember God's character and remind ourselves, "God is my heavenly Father, who cares for me. He is my Sovereign Lord who is larger than my problems, the Sufferer whose pain redeems this world."

Once we fill our minds with who God is, we can dwell on those thoughts. This is contemplation — sitting back and enjoying God in our hearts. In David's words, it is gazing upon God's beauty. His glory. His splendor. His loving, forgiving nature. His holiness. We just sit there and let the clock tick away. We sit and allow God's Spirit to remind us how Christ died for our sins ... and that God is calling us to a beautiful place ... and how we will live there in God's presence for eternity ... and what is there to fear? What is there to be afraid about, anyways?

We sit there and the words of a hymn might come to mind like:

> Amazing grace, how sweet the sound, that saved a wretch like me.... when we've been there ten thousand years, bright shining as the sun, there's no less days to sing God's praise than when we first begun.

As we think about those words and let them sink into our hearts, they affect us. Faith begins to replace fear. As we gaze upon the beauty of the Lord, we become changed.

Contemplation is a form of prayer in which we look upon God's face and gaze. We have already consciously laid down our problems and our fears that so easily distract us and instead we fill our minds with thoughts of God and dwell on that. Contemplation is a rich, spiritual habit. It is a perfect shelter for us when our perfect storms arise. And here's one way to do it . . .

FOCUS: Find a place of little distraction. Leave your problems, ignore any intruding thoughts and break through the "busy-ness barrier." Allow your heart to calm down. Confess what needs to be confessed. This may take just a few minutes, or much longer.

MEDITATE: Fill your mind with who God is. Study God's character, his words and his ways in the scriptures.

GAZE: Dwell on what you have learned about God's nature and ways. Be with God. Spend time thinking about what a wonderful God you have.

SOME PRACTICES IN CONTEMPLATIVE PRAYER

Those of us who practice contemplative prayer know that we're not there alone, but that *God is a part of the process.* There's an interaction that goes on as the Spirit of God may bring scriptures to mind or may speak to our sins, fears, doubts and despairs.

Commonly, in contemplative prayer, *the Spirit also gives us godly wisdom for our lives.* Back in Psalm 27, David prayed for God to guide his path as his enemies sought to destroy him. One misstep and they were sure to pounce. As he sought God, David asked God to give him the godly wisdom to escape. The same may happen to us as well during our times of contemplative prayer.

We can encourage one another through contemplative prayer. In one particular leadership crisis, I was preoccupied with worry. Then, a friend sat with me and reminded me who God is. This person read scripture after scripture to me about God's character and his ways. It was a kind of forced mediation, but it worked and snapped the cycle of worry.

We can also experience contemplative prayer together. A format may be for a group of friends to be with God alone in the morning, then to share and pray for each together over lunch. In the sharing, often there will be words of wisdom for each other that seem to come from God as a result of the contemplative hours.

The regular practice of contemplative prayer is invaluable for leaders during times of crisis. The Scriptures say in one place that, "David was greatly distressed because the men were talking of stoning him ... but David found strength in the LORD his God" (1 Samuel 30:6). In contemplative prayer, the Spirit speaks to our pain and fears and weaknesses and helps us to trust again in God's sufficiency.

When we gaze upon the beauty of the Lord, we have a perfect shelter for our perfect storms.

7

The Spiritual Disciplines

A disciple is a person who is under the discipline of another. As Christians, we are under Christ's discipline — that is, his training. He intends us to lead disciplined, trained lives in order to be productive for him.

Part of our training is to incorporate spiritual disciplines into our daily pattern of living. Some of the basic spiritual disciplines are being in fellowship, listening to preaching, reading the Bible and partaking of Holy Communion. In the late 20th century, Richard J. Foster introduced many Christians to other disciplines as well, including: fasting, meditation, study, solitude, submission, confession, worship, guidance, and celebration.

Since then, others have unearthed over sixty different disciplines, including "simplicity" and "silence" and even "unplugging" —which is disconnecting from technology to connect better with God. Today, a compilation of disciplines would also include such practices as:

Sabbath	Discipling	Hospitality
Retreat	Mentoring	Journaling
Slowing	Service	Memorization
Secrecy	Justice	Witnessing
Chastity	Examen	Bible Study

These are just a few of the training regimes that help us to grow in Christ. But we're not meeting together right now to review the different disciplines. Instead, we're here to find an overall philosophy to know how to use them in our lives. The best way to do this is to think through just what it means to be a disciple.

THE GRACEFUL ATHLETE

An image of discipleship that occurs in the scripture is that of an athlete. "Everyone who competes in the games goes into strict training," Paul writes in 1 Corinthians 9:25. The best athletes combine grace with effort, and the same holds true for disciples.

When our daughter was very young, we took her to learn to swim. Instead of swimming, she insisted on floating around the whole time and sucking her thumb! She had the grace, but not the effort. Needless to say, she only learned to swim much later. Sometimes we resemble that little girl in her swimming. We float around all our lives as disciples and make little effort to learn to swim.

In his invitation to discipleship, Jesus calls us to grace *and* effort:

> Come to me, all you who are weary and burdened, and I will give you rest. Take my yoke upon you and learn from me, for I am gentle and humble in heart, and you will find rest for your souls. For my yoke is easy and my burden is light. (Matthew 11:28-30)

Jesus is reassuring us that he is compassionate and understanding. If we follow him, he will train us according to our aptitudes. Under his *easy yoke* we must make an effort, yet it will also fit us correctly.

In the training which one man gave to his young horses, he first gently cared for them by brushing them, talking softly to them and giving them treats to eat. Then he gradually started leading them around. Only after he gained their trust and affection did he try to ride them. Gradually, they learned to love their new life since he fitted their training to their abilities and instincts.

A similar image of a grace-filled discipleship is seen in Mary of Bethany, who sat "at the Lord's feet listening to what he said" (Luke 10:39). When we adopt an attitude of "sitting and listening," Christ trains us under the easy yoke. He invites us to work alongside him and learn from him as a yoke-mate. It's a partnership in which he does most of the hard work. We feel his energy moving within us and motivating us, even as we serve him.

He may give us roles of service that challenge us, yet also match us.

Discipleship begins with grace and deepens with effort. We have to make lifestyle decisions, set goals and even decide if we want to suffer for Christ or not. Christ reminds us, "If anyone would come after me, he must deny himself and take up his cross and follow me" (Mark 8:34). Paul puts it adroitly: "work out your salvation with fear and trembling, for it is God who works in you to will and to act" (Philippians 2:12-13).

This is where the spiritual disciplines become important. They challenge us, prod us, remind us and enable us to grow spiritually. When we follow them, they turn us into graceful athletes

But here also lurks a danger.

The danger is when we begin to think of discipleship as "doing the disciplines," when it is not. The heart of discipleship must always remain grace. Spiritual disciplines are meant to enhance our love for God, not to replace that love. When they begin to exist for themselves, the yoke suddenly becomes burdensome.

This is what happened in the graceless version of discipleship offered by the Pharisees. They began around 150 BC as an irritant to an encroaching pagan Greek culture. Their primary teaching was that a believer must avoid "sinners." To do this, they cocooned themselves behind a defensive wall of rules and disciplines.

By the time of Jesus, the Pharisees had isolated themselves from practically everyone. They particularly despised the common people, who they called the "mob that knows nothing of the law — there is a curse on them" (John 7:49). The Pharisees sought to impose their iron-clad disciplines on them, but Jesus called them instead to his easy yoke.

We have a constant tendency to make our yokes heavier than they are meant to be. Consider it this way: when we first came to Christ, the discipleship software installed in our hearts ran just fine — Jesus 1.0. But then we read about new software that promised so much — Pharisee 2.0! When we installed it, however, our operating system began to run very slowly. That's what happens when we forget about grace. We need to uninstall the new software and go back to the original.

Christ was not a computer geek, but he did know about yokes, and he reminds us that our yokes are *custom-fitted*. We cannot wear another's yoke and expect it will not chafe. We cannot impose our yoke on someone else and think it will fit. Christ's custom-fitted yokes work perfectly, however. He is the Discipler, not we or someone else.

Our personalities certainly play a role in the custom-fitting. For instance, people with a rich imagination may benefit from doing the Ignatian exercises — in which they visualize themselves within a biblical story. Concrete thinkers, on the other hand, often find such exercises to be incomprehensible. They would prefer studying the Bible systematically.

Extroverts tend to pray aloud while introverts like quiet times of reflection. Since most leaders are extroverts, and most retreat leaders are introverts, this presents a problem. Retreats are often quiet and withdrawn affairs that convey the impression that only contemplative spirituality is correct. Retreat leaders need to be aware of the personalities of leaders and to be careful what they present as normative.

Personality tests, such as the Myers-Briggs Type Indicator (MBTI), help us to understand how our minds work. A number of authors, such as Reginald Johnson, have applied the results of MBTI testing to spirituality, suggesting the spiritual disciplines that best fit each personality.

Often, we already know what is best for us and need just a nudge to follow our instincts. On the other hand, sometimes we need a push into a new challenge. Having a coach can help, someone who will dare us to grow. This is the role of a spiritual director. He or she is not a manager, but someone who listens to God with us and helps us discern the working of the Spirit in our lives when we cannot alone. They help us reach beyond our own self-confining limits. Working with a spiritual director is yet another spiritual discipline.

In summary, grace and effort are both necessary to discipleship — grace begins discipleship and effort deepens it. To be graceful athletes, however, we must learn to balance the two.

IDENTITY THEFT

To use the spiritual disciplines properly, we also must be clear about our identity as disciples. Today, one of the greatest problems facing Christians is identity theft.

In the New Testament, the phrase "in Christ" occurs over 90 times to describe Christian discipleship. It is saying that a disciple is a person of such commitment that Christ has become their primary identity. In our lives, we have many identities — such as our family, ethnicity, politics, occupation or career. We cannot deny these associations, but a disciple is a person who finds their most important identity in Christ.

In 1987, the pollster George Gallup researched those who attend church. He was surprised to find "... little difference in ethical behavior between the churched and the unchurched. There's as much pilferage and dishonesty." [1]

Although the churched people followed the spiritual disciplines of listening to preaching, singing spiritual songs and partaking of Holy Communion, these had no effect on their conduct.

Gallup investigated further. It was only after he developed a way of measuring spiritual commitment that he discovered a difference in ethical behavior. Those who measured highest in spiritual commitment also had a much higher concern for improving society, were more tolerant, engaged in more charitable activities and were far happier than the rest.

Gallup's research shows that when Christianity is just a matter of custom or convenience for us, it makes little difference in our behavior. It does not matter what spiritual disciplines we follow, there also has to be a sincere personal decision to follow Christ wholeheartedly. Christ has to be our central identity.

As a scholarly monk, St. Jerome (347-420 AD) loved the Latin classical authors, especially Cicero. But his study began to affect his identity as a disciple. One night, Jerome had a vivid dream in

---

[1] "Vital Signs: An Interview with George H. Gallup" Leadership, Fall 1987.

which Christ appeared to him as a Judge. Christ asked Jerome, "Who are you?"

"I am a Christian," Jerome replied.

Christ retorted, "You're lying! You're a Ciceronian! Where your treasure is, there your heart will be also."

Jerome had lived by a number of spiritual disciplines as a monk, but that was not enough. His inordinate love of Cicero's words were endangering his commitment to Christ and his identity as a disciple.

Identity is a very important issue to leaders. We face many pressures within our organizations that can easily warp our sense of self. In our roles, we can begin defining ourselves by what we do, the power we possess or the title we have. Many of us particularly struggle with feelings of self-importance. When we see our name towards the top of an organizational chart, it makes us feel that we are better than others. Are we?

In many organizations, there is a power difference reinforced by a salary difference. It was refreshening once to be in an organization with equalized salaries — from the newest recruit to the executive. The absence of a hierarchal culture reinforced by salary differences broke down barriers and made us all feel equally important in our roles.

The ancient monks of the Egyptian desert felt self-importance to be one of the deadliest of sins. By it they meant the feeling of self-worth we derive by thinking we are better than others. Leaders who feed their egos too much fall prey to it.

Evagrios the Solitary advises how to drive away this demon. Do it, he said, "by intense prayer and by not doing or saying anything that contributes to the sense of your own importance."[2] Focus on Christ. Define yourself by what he did for you, rather than by what an organizational chart says.

Grace. Effort. Identity. Commitment. These are the elements that define what a disciple is. By settling these issues in our hearts, we will also gain a philosophy by which to use the spiritual disciplines profitably.

---

2   On Discrimination, 13.

8
Bible Reading as a Spiritual Discipline

Once I asked several hundred people in a survey the following questions: (1) "How much do you read the Bible?" and (2) "How close do you feel toward God?" In the survey, the more that people read the Bible, the closer they said they felt to God. The relationship proved linear: any increase in Bible reading was associated with a closer feeling to God.

Someone who heard about this survey decided to test it out. Without telling me, she read the Bible daily for a whole year and only then approached me. "For my whole life," she said, "I've attended church but never felt close to God. So, I started reading the Bible just like you said. And I honestly can say after one year that I found it to be true. For the first time, I now feel close to God!"

Of all the spiritual disciplines, Bible reading has been one of the most important in developing the spiritual life but it has fallen out of favor today since reading is a slow media. Many who try to read the Bible give up, saying that it's too confusing.

So, how can we read the Bible as a spiritual discipline?

WHAT IS THE BIBLE?

To read the Bible, we first must know what it is. At its simplest, **the Bible is the story of the self-revelation of God through a chosen people**. It was compiled over a thousand years and contains hundreds of individual stories, but the Bible always possesses this undeniable theme. It has a metanarrative — a Grand Story.

If you ever read Tolstoy's massive novel *War and Peace*, and someone asked you what it is about, there are several ways to answer. You might focus on the many individual stories about soldiers and their ladies. Or, thinking broader, you might say, "It concerns the Napoleonic Wars." The most expansive answer would try to understand what Tolstoy was saying about life when he wrote about war.

The Bible is like Tolstoy's *War and Peace* with its many plots and subplots. We can easily lose sight of the greater theme — the story of God's self-revelation to the world through a chosen people. When we understand this greater context, the individual stories of the Bible begin to make sense.

THE STORY OF GOD

There are many ways to trace the Story of God. The simplest is to follow the major events of the covenant between God and the chosen people. They are like stepping stones across the pages of the Bible:

CREATION: The Lord God created the world and established his reign in it, but humanity rejected its knowledge of God.

ABRAHAM: God made a covenant with Abraham and his descendants to reveal himself again to the world through them.

EXODUS: The descendants of Abraham became the people of Israel. God redeemed Israel from Pharaoh and reaffirmed his covenant with them as his chosen people.

NATIONHOOD: Israel became a nation under God's reign, but it failed to live for God or tell others what they learned about God.

EXILE: God sent his rebellious people into exile. The prophets predicted that a remnant would be restored under a righteous servant king who would bring in the true kingdom of God.

THE KINGDOM OF GOD: The promised restoration finally occurs in Jesus, the Messiah, who said at the beginning of his ministry, "The kingdom of God is at hand" (Mark 1:15).

In Jesus the self-revelation of God to the world is complete. Previously, the covenant people experienced God through word and event. Now they experienced him in the Son, "the exact representation of his being" (Hebrews 1:3). The Incarnation ties together all the loose ends of the Bible. It is the central interpretive principle of the Bible.

It is true that some secular scholars say the Bible is just a holy mash lacking a Story of God, divine revelation, or inspiration. But the love of God leads us to believe otherwise.

God is love, we are told (1 John 4:16). If this is so, would not God want us to know him? After all, that's what love does. It wants to know and be known. We believe in **revelation** because it is the Story which God told so we can know him.

The Story was told at the speed of people. God did not suddenly appear in the sky and command obedience. Instead, he called Abraham and his descendants to experience him in covenant. The chosen people wrote down their covenantal experiences of God and these writings became the Bible. We believe in the **inspiration** of the Bible because it is the record of the Story of God.

And this leads to the idea of **illumination**. It is the belief that, as we read the Bible, God speaks through it so we can understand his Story. He calls us to walk in a real-time covenant with him as disciples.

THE LITERAL READING OF THE BIBLE

Through the centuries, there have been two ways by which the Bible has been read. The first focuses on understanding the original background and meaning. This has been called the *literal reading* of the Bible. The other way reads the Bible devotionally to hear God, but often with little knowledge of the original customs and meaning. This devotional approach has been called the *spiritual reading* of the Bible.

Separately, the two approaches have their weaknesses. The literal reading of the Bible can be dry and lifeless while the spiritual reading of the Bible can cause us to read the Bible out of context. In fact, it produced centuries of fanciful, allegorical interpretations.

Today, it is clear: we need both study and devotion. A knowledge of the background enhances our devotional reading of the Bible and preserves us from fanciful interpretations.

We now have some excellent resources to help us read the Bible in context. Many study Bibles offer notes, introductions and paragraph titles that make reading far more productive and enjoyable. Handbooks and commentaries are also available.

The inductive method of Bible study is particularly helpful for exploring the background of a text while applying it to life. Often used in groups, an inductive approach first asks observation questions like: "Who is speaking?" "What is happening?" "When did it happen and where?" This leads to interpretive questions such as: "Why did it happen and how?" The final step probes the implications for our lives.

An even deeper study of the context of the Bible would involve learning the basic principles of biblical interpretation. Every serious Bible reader should study Fee and Stuart's *How to Read the Bible for All Its Worth* — or its equivalent. It describes the different literary genres within the Bible and how to interpret them.

THE DEVOTIONAL READING OF THE BIBLE

When most people read the Bible devotionally, they sit down, pray and then read "until the blessing comes." Once we know the background of a text, however, it enhances our devotional reading. We are better able to understand what the text originally meant and how to apply it in our lives.

Many people follow a devotional reading method known as *lectio divina* (LEX-i-oh di-VEE-nuh). It is when we read the scriptures slowly and prayerfully, paying special attention to the words that seem to jump out and speak to our lives. We then talk to God about our day in the light of what we learn and enjoy the spiritual words spoken to our souls.

Here is a brief outline of lectio divina as it has been commonly presented:

LECTIO DIVINA
Reading
Read a passage slowly in context.

Biblical Meditation
Mull over what seems meaningful.

Prayer
Pray about what you are meditating.

Contemplation
Abide with what speaks to your heart.

Some people like to add imagination to their devotional reading of the Bible by picturing themselves within a biblical story. For instance, we can daydream about being with Jesus in the boat on the Sea of Galilee. A storm arises and threatens the boat.

Close your eyes and think through the scene. Pretend that you are there in the boat. What do you experience? What are you feeling and thinking? How does it all speak to you?

Bible reading is one of the most valuable of all the spiritual disciplines. When we sense the Story of God, the Bible not only becomes less confusing, but it begins to affect us in a deeper way. When we understand the Bible in context, we are better equipped to hear it. And when we approach our Bible reading with a heart to love and obey God more, we become spiritually formed.

PART TWO
Becoming Authentic with People

9
Where Community Begins

Authenticity is an essential quality for a leader, perhaps the most significant of all, because leadership is so much about relationships. We cannot reach our fullest potential unless we are found trustworthy. When we lack authenticity, we are perceived as being hypocrites. The Greek word *hypokrites* is a fitting basis for the English *hypocrite*. It describes a play actor who struts on a stage and mouths a script. We may sound impressive, but we are not being real.

This book is about achieving authenticity as leaders. In the first section, we looked at becoming authentic with God. In the second, we will explore becoming authentic with people. The two are related: knowing God heals our relationships and helps us to form community.

GOD IS LOVE

Community begins with God. We say that "God is love" (1 John 4:16). By this we understand that the universe is not coldly mechanical by nature, nor is it ruled by a self-centered autocrat. Love and relationship lie at the very heart of everything. Community exists within the very being of God.

This is not to say there is more than one God, since there is not. Rather, it is to realize that God is not a mere force or the Great Alone One. Within God there is a constant expression of love, involving relatedness and genuineness, knowing and being known. God is a Community of Love.

The New Testament describes this relatedness within God as the Father, Son and Holy Spirit — what would later be called the Holy Trinity. In the fourth century, the Cappadocian Fathers beautifully depicted the constant expression of Eternal Love within the Trinity as a Holy Dance that is endless and harmonious, united yet distinct — each member of the Trinity serving and honoring the other.

The communal nature of God becomes the basis of Christian community. When we know God, we want to imitate God's relatedness with each other. We rejoice and mourn together, devote ourselves to one another and honor one another above ourselves. As we serve each other and bear each other's burdens, we become one body.

Our personal experience of God influences how we treat each other. As Paul wrote:

If you have any encouragement from being united with Christ, if any comfort from his love, if any fellowship with the Spirit, if any tenderness and compassion, then make my joy complete by being like-minded, having the same love, being one in spirit and purpose. (Philippians 2:1-2)

Knowing God and knowing each other, we become more authentic as people and as leaders.

THE HOLY TRINITY AND LEADERSHIP

In 2 Corinthians 13:14, Paul gives us a trinitarian blessing:

"May the grace of the Lord Jesus Christ,
the love of God,
and the fellowship of the Holy Spirit
be with you all."
(2 Corinthians 13:14).

It summarizes how the Trinity touches us: as we experience the grace, love and fellowship of God. When we encounter God like this in our lives, it will affect how we lead.

The Grace of Christ

Christ's death reconciles us to God. This makes us become more authentic as leaders by crafting us into people of grace and by imparting a redemptive quality to our relationships. We want to forgive and bless in return.

Many organizations have a *utilitarian* view of people — they use people and then discard them when they no longer fulfill the purposes of the organization. But when we experience the grace of Jesus, it changes our attitude toward people from *utilitarian* to *redemptive*. Instead of asking, "How can I use people for my purposes?" we begin thinking, "How can I develop people as we work together?" Living in God's grace, we learn to offer grace to others.

This is an important cultural implication of Christianity for leaders. Because Christ shed his blood for us, we know that human life is valuable. Ultimately, this simple fact prompts us to develop policies in our organizations that treat people with respect and dignity.

The Love of God the Father

God the Father loves the world he created. He is leading and guiding it toward an ultimate destiny. We can be a part of God's work by following Christ. When we do so, Paul says, "The Spirit himself testifies with our spirit that we are God's children" (Romans 8:16). God whispers into our hearts that we belong to him.

When we personally realize that we are loved by God our Father, this becomes the foundation of our lives. It makes us more authentic as people by replacing our insecurities and excessive desire for money, power and fame. It heals our lives and our relationships.

One study done at Rush University Medical Center in Chicago demonstrates the power of the love of God. In the study, patients who strongly knew that God loved them were 75 percent more likely to get better with medical treatment for clinical depression. Researcher Patricia Murphy said this was "tied specifically to the belief that a Supreme Being cared." [1]

Nurturing ourselves in the love of God is more important than we may realize. Years ago, an elderly Christian doctor spoke these unforgettable words to me over and over: "One thing I have learned is always to remember to love God every day. Love God and be loved by God. That is the most important thing of all." That is the main point behind a daily devotional time: to allow time to nurture ourselves in the love of God.

The Fellowship of the Spirit

When we become disciples, the Holy Spirit of God comes to live within us. At various times, the Spirit will providentially encourage, empower, prod, pull and guide us toward the destiny which God has prepared for us in Christ. We experience

---

1   News release from Rush University Medical Center, 23 February 2010.

the Spirit directly and also through each other in Christ.

The fellowship we have with the Spirit affects how we treat others. In imitation of the Spirit, we will find ourselves encouraging, empowering, mentoring and guiding others toward their fulfillment.

Mentoring is one way by which we particularly imitate the Spirit. It is the process by which we turn others into leaders. In mentoring, we offer our wisdom and valuable time for the benefit of another instead of pursuing our own goals. It is one of the most selfless and godly ways a leader can exhibit the character of God.

CONCLUSION

The communal nature of God is the basis of Christian community. Knowing God, we desire community. Experiencing the Trinity, we find ourselves treating those we lead differently.

Sadly, most leaders have never experienced fellowship in depth and have no idea of its power to affect their lives. Although the desire for community exists within us, so do all our natural hesitations against it. In the next two chapters we will explore how to go deeper in Christian community.

10
Picturing Community
Dr. Harvey Shepard

We have just considered how authenticity comes from God and how we grow in authenticity by experiencing God in a Christian fellowship. But what should such a spiritual community look like for us here and now?

Many are unsure. Someone expressed, "I know community when I've experienced it, but I don't think I can describe it." It is important to learn what community looks like, for one goal of leaders should be to nurture it.

It is important to understand that Christian community is not an option. While in this book we are considering going deeper with God and going deeper with people separately, they in reality occur simultaneously. These two tasks are fulfillments of the two greatest commandments, and neither one is accomplished without doing the other. We cannot love God fully unless we love our neighbor, and vice versa.

Dietrich Bonhoeffer learned much about Christian community leading an underground seminary prior to his execution near the end of the Second World War. He reminds us that we do not create Christian community, but already possess it *in Christ*, who establishes and holds it together. Although Christian community is ours as a gift, we must learn to recognize and nurture it.

TWO PICTURES

If Bonhoeffer was right, and we already have community, why is it often so difficult to see, if not at times unpleasant to participate in?

We must remember that our Christian experience has been aptly described by the phrase "Already, Not Yet." This highlights a tension in each aspect of our faith: that we *already* have a relationship with God and participate in his kingdom, but that there is more awaiting us – the *not yet*.

Community is like this as well. It is already there, but it is not yet all that it can become. As we develop a picture of community it must reflect this "Already, Not Yet" paradox. It needs to reflect both where we are, and where we are headed.

Scripture provides us with two pictures that capture this "Already, Not Yet" tension which together give us a more complete appreciation of what Christian community looks like. The first picture is the Garden from Genesis 1-2. The second picture is people becoming family to one another.

Both pictures possess aspects of "Already, Not Yet" because we are on a journey – established by God and heading toward fullness in Him. This journey is transformational, for it takes inherently self-centered individuals and forms them into a community that reflects the beauty of God to the world around them. Christian community is re-creation; people becoming family and returning to the Garden together.

THE GARDEN

The Garden shows us how things were meant to be, and explains what went wrong. The Garden was a place of intact relationships — with God, self, others, and the created world. Returning to the Garden involves each of these broken relationships being restored in Christ. Recall that at the heart of the Garden is the eternal love of the Trinity. This love is always inviting us deeper into relational wholeness – not just in our relationship with God, but in all areas of our brokenness.

When it comes to relationships with others in community, Bonhoeffer uses the image of *Christ between us*. Christ stands between us and all others, so that He is the ultimate *other* for any

Christian in community. Therefore, as we view others we are reminded that they are forgiven in Christ, no matter how offensive they might otherwise be to us – we treat them as we would treat Christ. Likewise, as we consider others looking at us, we realize that our identity is not in ourselves. Our worth is in Christ alone. Christ between us reminds us how Christ becomes the mediator not just between a person and God, but between people.

The healing love of God found in the Garden restores not only our relationship with God and with others, but also with ourselves. True growth in our knowledge of God will go hand in hand with a deeper knowledge of self – what some theologians have called "Double Knowledge." God's healing love requires a willingness on our part to be open and vulnerable.

In this journey we begin moving from a false identity of self-sufficiency towards a true-self of brokenness before God and one another. The integrity and authenticity of the Garden means that who we are is no longer dependent upon what we do or our position, but it is more fully rooted in Christ. This can be very threatening, especially for an individualistic leader. David Benner, a Christian psychologist and spiritual formation author reminds us, "To know that I am loved, I must accept the frightening helplessness and vulnerability that is my true state. This is always terrifying."

In the Garden Adam and Eve were naked and not ashamed. For us in the reality of our "Not Yet" state, our brokenness becomes our nakedness. Here, of course, community plays a significant role. Community often is where our brokenness comes to the surface, and community is the place where the love of Christ is extended to us as part of our healing.

We cannot avoid the poverty of our souls if we desire transformation.

Jean Vanier, founder of L'Arche, a community dedicated to caring for those with developmental disabilities, highlights this: "Once you have realized [your own brokenness], either you run away or else you have to come to terms with it, with the help of brothers and sisters in community and with the help of God. The love and support of community gives you the certitude you are loved just as you are, with all your wounds...." [1]

The Garden reminds us that community can be a place where our relationship with creation is renewed. We tend to take for granted that the Garden was a place of beauty and creativity.

---

1 Jean Vanier, From Brokenness to Community (Paulist Press, New York, 1992), 19-20.

Community should be a place where our own group creativity reflects the beauty of the garden. The possibilities are endless: music, visual arts, apartment decor, gardening, enjoying a park or the mountains together for a day, poetry, and so on.

In other words, community should not be limited to Bible studies and shared meals — it should be a creative expression of who God has made us to be, together helping recreate the beauty of the Garden as a reflection of the beauty of God. Our community will then become a restorative place that is inviting to others.

THE FAMILY

We've seen where we are headed, toward the re-creation of the Garden. But what about the nitty-gritty "not yet" and brokenness of everyday life? We now turn our attention to the second image of community, the family, an image so rich in application that the church is referred to as the family of God.

Community occurs among people who put the principles we discussed from the Garden into action and become family to one another. Some of us have come from family relationships that were wonderful, and a few of us from those that were horrible, but most of our natural families are in the vast in between. We will take a few minutes to look at what makes up healthy families, and see how those principles nurture community.

Families are characterized by *stability and intimacy*. In other words, members know what to expect from one another, and they are relationally close. Such relationships are formed by covenants, not contracts.   It is important to appreciate the difference. Covenants are offered freely, and focus more on what one will give than what one will receive.   Birthed in love and offered freely, covenants may be one-way at first, with the hope of maturing from unilateral to bilateral. Contracts, on the other hand, ensure that we will get what we want from a relationship – thus they belong in the realm of business, not family.

Families share *rituals*, and these contribute to how families develop a sense of connectedness. Perhaps some holidays are celebrated together in a certain way. Birthdays or other special events are shared. Perhaps it's two 'brothers' sharing coffee together every Thursday morning. These rituals add to the stability as well as the fun of being family to one another.

Most families are also *intergenerational*, and this serves as an important reminder when it comes to being in community. We don't need communities where everyone else is just like us, but we need to have people that function like a father, mother, brother, sister, aunt or uncle – and we need to play those roles ourselves in the lives of others.

You may be recognizing that both images of community – the Garden and the Family – have *costs*. People will see us at our worst! There will be the cost of exposure – and the cost of bearing the burden of loving others, in Christ, in spite of their brokenness. Vulnerability may seem threatening, but it is a catalyst for community. Brokenness creates a sense of safety: that it is acceptable to not be perfect, and opens the opportunity for healing.

Lastly, families are places of *hospitality*. Hospitality is particularly important for Christian community because it draws others in. Hospitality is superior to generosity because it is more invasive – hospitality draws others into places in our lives that are personal and of great value to us. But it also gives others an opportunity to see who God is.

It's just as Jesus reminded us, "By this all people will know that you are my disciples, if you have love for one another" (John 13:35). And he also prayed: "… that they may all be one, just as you, Father, are in me, and I in you, that they also may be in us, so that the world may believe that you have sent me" (John 17:21).

SOME DANGEROUS TENDENCIES

These two images, the Garden and the Family, give us a good picture of community – helping us recognize what community looks like so that we can nurture it. But there are several warnings to be sounded.

First, it is easy to idealize community. Community, in those moments, is a place of feeling good all the time, a place of acceptance where (completely unrealistically) we will never be found to be lacking Christian virtue and maturity, adored by all and satisfied with each day's activities.

That is the place of dreams, not of the "Already, Not Yet"! But community is not the place of dreams, it is something far better. Community is the place of being changed. The transformation that happens within community comes as it does to a seed, which must die and be buried for new life to come forth.

Being in community is painful, and our ego has to die. Vanier reminds us that we will only tolerate that recurring pain if we realize being in community isn't just a preference we choose, but a part of our obedience to God. He writes: "We will only stay in community if we have gone through the passage from choosing community to knowing that we have been chosen for community." [2] Community is part of our calling, and at times it will be painful.

Likewise, just as there is a tendency to idealize community, there is the danger of expecting some *particular* experience of it – for community to be predictable. Bonhoeffer understood this, warning that even though we all at some time or another have been encouraged by the *experience* of genuine Christian community, we err if we make that particular experience the norm. "We have no claim upon such experiences, and we do not live with other Christians for the sake of acquiring them.... We are bound together by faith, not by experience." [3]

Lastly, living in community is a call to focused living in the moment. Our tendency, however, is to live worried over the past or anxious about the future, but community happens now – in the current moment. For many of us, perhaps especially visionary leaders, it is hard to not see 'now' as a stepping stone for something later. But this does not nurture community – it instead risks using people as stepping stones to accomplish your agenda – and may leave others lying in the path

---

2 Vanier, pg. 40.

3 Dietrich Bonhoeffer, Life Together (Harper & Row Publishers, New York, 1954), 39.

behind you unable to participate in true community.

People becoming family and returning to the Garden fully engaged in the moment and not idealizing community or demanding a particular experience of it – this is the journey of community. Often our community will have a few members with whom we are particularly close – just as Jesus had Peter, James and John in the midst of the Twelve Apostles and the even bigger group of his followers. Those in this inner circle, our covenant group, are those with whom we share our most intimate experience of community.

11
Covenant Groups

In his book, *Authentic Leadership*, Bill George writes as a corporate leader of his long-term participation in a spiritual group with other corporate leaders. Many Christian leaders quietly participate in such groups.

In this chapter, we will describe one type of spiritual group for leaders, a covenant group — what it is and how to form one.

WHAT IS A COVENANT GROUP?

A covenant group is a small group characterized by mutually accountable relationships for spiritual formation. It is more than a study group or a coffee klatch, but an attempt to form a true community where we can be open about ourselves and offer God's grace to one another as we grow in Christ.

In a covenant group, we agree to go beyond "pseudo-community" in favor of walking deeply together. A Christian fellowship is meant to be a family that has the power to redeem us from the scars of our past. When we have close spiritual friends in our lives — people with whom we can laugh, play, eat, cry and pray together — we immediately see the difference it makes and desire it for ourselves.

The New Testament describes Christian fellowship as rich and deep and full of such reciprocal actions as:

- Accepting one another
- Agreeing with one another
- Being kind to one another
- Being hospitable to one another
- Bearing one another's burdens
- Caring for one another
- Encouraging one another
- Forgiving one another
- Honoring one another
- Laying down our lives for one another
- Living in harmony with one another
- Loving one another
- Speaking truthfully to one another
- Teaching and admonishing one another

Many leaders have never experienced spiritual fellowship like this, so they have no idea of its value. Yet, when we do experience authentic Christian community, we know how it can change us by healing our human brokenness.

Where do we find such a fellowship? A church would be a good place to start. Many churches now have small group ministries to help people go deeper with each other in fellowship.

But a covenant group for leaders is a unique breed. It is not just another small group, but a covenanted circle in which people agree to walk together. It requires a certain degree of vulnerability and openness. The participants should have an awareness of what it means to be leader, if they are not all leaders themselves. And there has to be trust. Such groups are not often found within churches. We may have to form a covenant group ourselves from a few like-minded friends.

The heart of such a group is its covenant. This need not be formally written out, but it should be clearly understood. It answers the question, "How will we walk together to form community and grow in Christ?" Everyone must whole-heartedly desire to have these two goals in their lives.

Covenant groups come in a variety of forms. The simplest is just to meet together to share the joys and struggles of being a disciple. Some covenant groups also practice a spiritual discipline together, like studying the Bible, reading Christian authors, or being involved in a social justice project — in addition to their regular personal sharing about their discipleship. If a group lasts for years, members might periodically re-invent their covenant to explore new ways of being together.

Covenant groups can differ by culture. People share more freely with their peers in an egalitarian culture. But in some cultures, personal matters tend to be discussed in private with an older, spiritual leader rather than in a group of peers. Each covenant group must work out how its members will form community and grow in Christ.

Forming a covenant group among leaders may take time since we are so good at building walls to hide behind. It took one group of leaders I know several years before they could talk honestly about themselves. Eventually, all of these people did become close friends and they eagerly looked forward to meeting every week. What made the difference for them was a facilitator who gradually helped them to develop trust.

In the long run, a covenant group will only work if we allow ourselves to be known. We have to leave our pretenses aside. This means, when we tell our life stories, we will include our sorrows as well as our joys. We will mention our failures, temptations and struggles, and not just the triumphs. We will not leave out talking about our human brokenness and may even be willing to admit to our doubts and fears and true motives. There has to be vulnerability.

There can be vulnerability when there is trust and love. A covenant group is meant to be a redemptive refuge in which we watch over each other. In it, we will do nothing to hurt or reject another. Instead, we know that love "always protects, always trusts, always hopes, always perseveres" (1 Corinthians 13:7). Like caring siblings, we will listen to each other, hold each other accountable and speak the truth to one another in love.

It takes time to develop friendships like these, and it requires a commitment to continue them. Covenant groups make us less independent and more inter-dependent. Living for one another may even mean we change our lifestyles for each other. Some of us will find this difficult to do and will drop-out. The benefit of a covenant group comes, however, for those who want to grow close.

Just as the Lord God said that it was not good for Adam to be alone, the same is true for Christian leaders. We are meant to share our lives together. Being part of a covenant group can help us do that.

12

Collegial and Hero Leadership

L eadership is built on relationships. We see this clearly in Jesus' own leadership team, the Twelve Apostles. Jesus developed his team around four core leaders whom he knew personally and who also knew each other well.

Matthew mentions the day when Jesus formed the core of his team:

> He saw two brothers, Simon called Peter and his brother Andrew. They were casting a net into the lake, for they were fishermen. "Come, follow me," Jesus said, "and I will make you fishers of men." (Matthew 4:18-19)

A verse later, Jesus calls James and John who immediately "left the boat and their father and followed him" (Matthew 4:22).

Matthew gives us the impression that Jesus just walked up to four strangers, commanded them to follow him and they did so. What Matthew does not tell us is Jesus' prior relationship with these men.

James and John were Jesus' first cousins.

Mary, the mother of Jesus, was sister to Salome, the mother of James and John (cf. Matthew 27:56, Mark 16:1, John 19:25). This is why, when Jesus was dying on the cross, he asks John to take care of Mary, his aunt (John 19:26-27). Normally, such a request was made only of a close family member.

Furthermore, James, John and Peter were in business together (Luke 5:10).

In other words, Jesus formed the core of his leadership team around four men whom he knew and who knew each other very well. In fact, of all of the Twelve Apostles, we read of Jesus giving nicknames only to James, John and Peter. He calls Peter, "*Rocky*," and his cousins, James and John, the "*Sons of Thunder*." Cousins have been called a lot worse!

These men became Jesus' his closest confidants. At times, we read how he gave exclusive access only to "Peter, James and John" (Luke 8:51, 9:28). John seems to be the closest of all.

Some say that a leader should not become personal friends with the people he or she leads. Apparently, this was not so with Jesus. He knew that leadership depends on relationships. He was personal friends with the people he led, but he also knew when to act with authority toward them. That's where the difference lies.

Further evidence suggests that Jesus divided the Twelve even more into teams, with the team leaders being Peter, Philip and James the son of Alphaeus. Scholars deduce this from the various lists of the apostles, where the first, fifth and ninth names are always the same, implying grouping. On mission assignments, we also read how that the apostles were sent out "two by two" (Mark 6:7, Luke 10:1).

WHAT THIS TELLS US

Jesus' organization of the Twelve tells us two important things. First and foremost, Jesus wanted his apostles to function as colleagues, not as individuals. He did not call his apostles into loneliness. He called them into a relationship with other apostles.

Secondly, Jesus created structures for the support and accountability of his teams. He sent the apostles out in pairs and appears to have used teams of four. There was a deliberate attempt to provide encouragement, accountability and development. Jesus expected his apostolic leaders to grow as disciples and to care about their brother apostles.

As a result, when the apostles founded churches, they adopted the same collegial model of leadership they learned from Christ. The apostles made decisions together (Acts 2:42-47; 15:1-29).

They taught that a church is the "body of Christ" in which all the members are important and bear responsibility for each other (Romans 12:3-8, 1 Corinthians 12). They also ordained elders and deacons to serve together as collegial leaders in local churches.

It is obvious that Jesus taught a collegial model of Christian leadership and that the earliest disciples adopted it and incorporated it into the church.

COLLEGIAL AND HERO LEADERSHIP

Besides the collegial model of leadership, Christ also exemplified heroic leadership. Hero leaders are willing to go against the crowd, live a life of endurance for others and suffer personally. It says that Jesus "endured the cross, scorning its shame" (Hebrews 12:2). Similarly, we are to deny ourselves, take up our crosses and follow him (Mark 8:34).

Since Christ exemplifies both collegial and hero leadership, this suggests the ideal of Christian leadership must be a blend of the two. We are meant to be strong, sacrificial leaders who also know how to work intentionally together as a team.

This is the ideal. However, ideals easily can become distorted.

In the past, many Christian leaders have tended to over-emphasize the heroic aspects of Christian leadership. J. Oswald Sanders' seems to do this in his classic book, *Spiritual Leadership*. He portrays leaders almost exclusively as individualistic heroes, but never once as part of a collegium. This may explain why he tells us that leaders are *meant* to be lonely:

> From its very nature, the lot of the leader must be a lonely one. He must always be ahead of his followers. ... In his journey to the top he had left behind all his contemporaries and stood alone in the mount with his God. ... It is often heartbreaking to have to make decisions of far-reaching importance which affect the lives of loved fellow workers — and to make them alone. [1]

Such a version of hero leadership is attractive to leaders who are individualistic or proud, or who come from cultures that glorify the hero leader, but it is an unbalanced form of leadership. It leads to over-functioning, micro-managing and dependencies. It makes us feel we are indispensable and that chronic fatigue is a virtue when it is not. It leads to burn out, or causes a family member to "act out."

---

1 J. Oswald Sanders, Spiritual Leadership (1967), page 107.

When we lead like this, we may be bowing to our own idols. Leadership is not about fulfilling our need to feel like a hero. It is about loving and serving God.

Of course, *collegial* leadership also can become unbalanced. A leadership team can degenerate into a group of insipid chums who hesitate to take initiative on their own and do not even want to debate one another vigorously, less it impair the nice atmosphere.

The ideal that Christ has modeled for us is a collegial leadership composed of heroes. We are meant to be strong, sacrificial leaders who know how to work together.

To do this we must be strong yet humble. We must be capable of self-initiative yet also able to work in community. Such an ideal of leadership takes time to develop, especially if it runs counter to expectation. In the end, however, it is a healthier form of leadership that Jesus himself practiced and is worthy to emulate.

13

Solitude and Community

One night, I was in an ocean resort town where I was conversing with a friend about his life. As we talked, we went on a pier that jutted far into the ocean. Looking back at the town from a distance, we saw it for what it was —a gaudy strip of carnival stores hugging the shore line. There, you could throw darts for prizes, or get your face painted. The resort stretched out before us in Vanity Fair makeup as we talked about life and Christ. Somehow, just our simple action of withdrawing gave us the perspective we needed to think about eternity. Solitude is like that. It is withdrawing to see the whole picture and our place in it.

It may seem strange to include a chapter on solitude in a broader section on "Becoming Authentic with People," yet as Richard Foster once wrote, "Solitude can often heighten our understanding of those we love most."

Solitude provides clarity to our relationships with God and others. Solitude increases solidarity.

If solitude were just self-centeredness, it would be incompatible with community. But true solitude is not like that. When we meet God in our solitude, we receive two gifts for our relationships with others: the gift of compassion and the gift of perspective.

THE GIFT OF COMPASSION

Solitude renews our love for God and people. The Apostle John warns, "Dear children, keep yourselves from idols" (1 John 5:21). He was talking about the things that dull love: "If anyone loves the world, the love of the Father is not in him" (1 John 2:15).

The world is full of glitzy idols, especially for leaders. We have our desires and goals and secretly gloat about our achievements and power. It is only when we periodically get away from it all that we can see clearly. In solitude, we come clean and "de-idolize" ourselves.

Before Thomas Merton entered into one particular period of solitude, he said he despised the world. After he emerged from solitude, he wondered if he would still have the same feelings. Instead, he found solitude had the following effect on him:

> I met the world and I found it no longer so wicked after all. Perhaps the things I had

resented about the world when I left it were defects of my own that I had projected upon it. Now, on the contrary, I found that everything stirred me with a deep and mute sense of compassion. [1]

When solitude lessens our attraction for the world's idols, our compassion for others will grow since we become less occupied with ourselves.

THE GIFT OF PERSPECTIVE

Solitude not only increases our compassion for people, it also gives us the gift of perspective.

Over the long-run, one of the greatest dangers in leadership is to lose perspective. The continuing obligations and daily routines, the tyranny of the urgent, the boredom and the monotony of leadership all subtly yet surely change us over time until we forget our vision and true priorities toward others. Practicing the rhythms of solitude helps us to maintain our perspective.

When we first start out as leaders, we tend to have the mind of a sprinter who runs in brilliant bursts of energy. With time, we learn that leadership is really more of a long-distance run, not a sprint.

---

1 Thomas Merton, The Sign of Jonas (Harcourt Brace & Co., New York, 1953; First Harvest edition, 1981), pp. 91-92.

As much as eighty percent of the running muscles of an Olympic sprinter are "fast-twitch" fibers that are *glucose-burning*, producing quick bursts of energy in a dash. In contrast, as much as eighty percent of the running muscles of an Olympic marathoner are composed of "slow-twitch" fibers — which burn *oxygen* for a slower yet more consistent energy output.

If we are to be a deep person in leadership, sooner or later we have to change our thinking from sprinting to long-distance running. When we are sprinting, we simply do not realize how limited our burst of energy will be. When we begin marathoning, we do not realize just how far we truly can run. Indeed, this is why we tend to overestimate what we can accomplish in a year and underestimate what we can accomplish in five.

The rhythms of solitude, then, are more important than we might realize at first. In fact, when we are thinking like sprinters, solitude seems like a ridiculous interruption — a worthless pause in the race. Perhaps we can begin to understand why the Benedictines went so far as to *plan* their holy pauses to fall every few hours, with bells interrupting urgencies, so they could mingle their being with their doing. Their pauses were stepping stones through their day to check their hearts. If you will, they regarded prayer to be the greater urgency for their lives.

I once knew a school principal who knew everyone by name — students, parents and staff. He genuinely cared for each of these people. In return, to put it mildly, everyone loved him. I asked him one day, "What's your secret? What makes you like this?" He replied simply, "For the last twenty years, I've been reading the Bible every day. I think that made the difference." Little did he know that he was following his own version of the old Benedictine daily rhythm of work and prayer. As a leader, he was running like a long-distance monk.

Like this principal, many leaders have learned the value of practicing a daily solitude. The scriptures do not dictate to us the exact form this solitude should take, but they do remind us to dwell on God's everlasting presence every day.

On a weekly basis, Sabbaths also deepen the gift of perspective within us by rudely interrupting the mundane. Each new Sabbath stands at our door to announce, "Life is not all work." Sabbaths quell our inner compulsions and renew our love for God and neighbor. Once a week, when we let the world go on without us, we learn how to play in God's providential care.

Beyond these daily and weekly rhythms of solitude, we can also develop other rhythms on our own — which may take the form of a monthly retreat, or a yearly review. There is no rule about it. Each of us finds the patterns of solitude which best suit our own needs and goals.

As we practice solitude periodically, we gain both compassion and perspective, thereby increasing our ability to discern what is truly important in our relationships.

PART THREE

Becoming Spiritual in Leadership

14

The Spirit by Which We Lead

We have been developing the thought that godly leadership forms as we become authentic with God and with people. Out of this authenticity, we begin to lead others in a spiritual way.

For the last section of this book, we will linger on that last note — on the spirit by which we lead. To do so properly, we need to reach back in time — to the desert fathers and mothers of the third and fourth centuries. They were the true, deep-person leaders. Although none of them held a position of power, their influence continues even to the present day.

SHENOUDA'S DREAM

The desert fathers were Coptic Christians. It was my priviledge to serve the Coptic Orthodox Church for a number of years as a language teacher. In my time, Shenouda III was the leader of the Coptic Church.

One night, Shenouda had a dream in which he was taken to heaven and the angels showed him a beautiful city where the "ministers of God dwelt." A young man at the time, Shenouda had been a rising star in his world. He led effectively and efficiently as a church leader, but he was also mechanical and lacking in feeling.

In the dream, an angel sternly told him he could not enter the beautiful city. "You are not, in God's judgment, a minister," the angel said.

The angel began confronting Shenouda for his self-absorption and his lack of love for God and people. Shenouda was told such things as:

> Love is the main basis for ministry. Unless you love those whom you minister to, you will not be able to serve them and unless they love you, they will not benefit from you.

In the end, Shenouda is told he has made his choices. His life has ended and he cannot go back. When he hears this verdict, he desperately cries out the words, "I want another chance! I want another chance!" Calling out like this for a long time in his dream, he awoke and found himself again in his room, a second chance granted. [1]

---

1   The story is in Shenouda's book, published in Egypt, The Release of the Spirit.

Shenouda says this was the true beginning of his leadership, when he learned the importance of the spirit by which we lead. In later years, Shenouda would write that leadership "... is not just an activity but a spirit transferred from one person to another ... it is a life which the person ministered to absorbs." Shenouda's dream reflects the tradition of desert spirituality of his Coptic forebears.

For all leaders, the lesson is the same: it's not just what we do that counts; it's also who we are as a person that makes the difference in leadership.

THE EGYPTIAN DESERT

The silence lies heavy in the desert of Egypt . . . so heavy, with no modern mechanical interruptions, nor natural motion of trees, not even the whisper of a breath of wind, that it just develops its own presence. In the desert, the silence is engulfing, so thick that talking seems like an act of violence, like shattering a piece of glass. Being alone in the desert, the loudest sound is the beating of the heart and the Brownian motion of molecules on your eardrum. In this setting, the desert fathers and mothers went to hear the voice of God.

They did so as their world was changing. Pagan Rome was crumbling to the touch of Christianity, but the new faith was also losing its virulence. As conversions to Christ became *avant garde*, the church became increasingly shallow. This caused men and women who hungered for God to drift into the desert, where they could be deep people on their own terms.

The desert fathers and mothers became the spiritual leaders of their time. They remembered Jesus' words, "You are the salt of the earth," and became living reminders of what true salt was supposed to taste like in a world gone insipid.

They left behind for us specific instructions on how to produce holy salt for ourselves — instructions on spiritual formation that they summed up by a single Greek word, *theosis*.

What is theosis?

It is becoming holy by having a Holy Christ form within us. Athanasius (293-373 AD) describes it in the catchy phrase, "God became man in order that man might become God."[2] He was not saying that we become God, only that Christ can form within us. It is participating "in the divine nature" to "escape the corruption in the world" (1 Peter 1:3-4). It is a sword laying in God's flame: the sword glowing from the fire but not becoming the fire.

---

2 Athanasius, <u>On the Incarnation of the Word</u>, 54.3. The concept also is in Irenaeus.

The desert monks used theosis to produce holy salt. They fasted. They prayed. Some lived deep in the desert, completely alone. They reflected extensively about their struggle and eventually formed a theory of spiritual formation. They thought of it as a war in which the grace of God vanquishes our prevailing sins, one by one.

Evagrius Ponticus (345-399 AD), interviewed these trailblazing monks and wrote down their thoughts. St. John Cassian, who stayed with the desert monks between 385 and 399 A.D., also listened and promoted their thoughts in the western Roman Empire. Eventually, Cassian's formulation became the famous seven deadly sins: pride, gluttony, lust, envy, anger, greed and sloth.

The desert fathers and mothers regarded these sins as *passions* —impulses that enslave us and make us passive to their will. They taught that when we yield to these passions, we become slaves of the demonic, gratifying "the cravings of our sinful nature and following its desires and thoughts" (Ephesians 2:1-3). Spiritual formation is a process by which God gradually drives out these prevailing sins through grace.

WALKING THE ANCIENT PATH

So, how do we walk this ancient path today? First, we must recognize that the desert fathers and mothers were tough desert fighters who were waging a fierce spiritual war. Walking the ancient path is to journey into a spiritual battle.

The desert dwellers would tell us that the very first thing is to repent in a heartfelt way — to turn from all the sins we know about in our lives. They would not have understood blithe talk about "accepting Jesus" unless it also included a soulful reconciliation with God.

Repentance is difficult, but necessary — like the butterfly which must wriggle out of its cocoon to live. Unless we wriggle out of ourselves through repentance, we will never be able to live for God.

If one does escape the cocoon of self, the next task is to become watchful for temptation.

The Salts warn us to keep watch and pray. They regarded temptation as a demonic provocation, a military feint, to deceive and entrap us. They kept a wary eye on the Other Side and developed their own working knowledge on how to respond. If we assent to sin, it will deceive and enslave us. If we resist a provocation, we will become spiritually stronger and more discerning.

That was how they fought — Salts vs. Demons — except we should mention one thing: the Salts played dirty against the Demons. They had a secret weapon, which they called *asceticism*. The monks asked, "If Jesus battled the demons by fasting, why can't we?"

"Asceticism" comes from *askesis*, the Greek word for athletic exercising. It is the use of the spiritual disciplines of weakness — such as fasting or keeping vigil — to make ourselves more dependent on God's grace. It fulfills Paul's insight: "When I am weak, then I am strong" (2 Corinthians 12:10, cf. I Cor 9:24-27).

The goal of Christian asceticism is to develop a life of prayer. The goal is not to denigrate the body, as many commonly misunderstand. Since God declared the material world to be good in creation, the body cannot be evil. Ascetic spiritual disciplines are simply a means to help us grow closer to God.

The monks noticed, as they grew in prayer and gradually became free from their inner passions, that a deep quietness and peace began to permeate their lives. They became dispassionate in the sense that they were liberated from their demonic passions. Their souls were freer to love God. The Greek Orthodox Church calls this inner stillness, *hesychia*. It's a form of prayer when we live in communion with God, free from life's idolatries. It is a state of inner tranquility marked by quietly abiding in God.

In this state of deep trust and inner quiet, we grow in spiritual discernment. We become able to hear the voice of God and distinguish it from the self and Satan. Antony the Great (251-356 AD), the practical founder of the ancient desert movement, considered discernment to be the most important of all the Christian virtues since it makes all the other virtues possible.

But here lies the paradox: to *become* spiritually discerning, we also need to *be* discerning. Since no one possesses spiritual wisdom in the beginning of the journey of spiritual formation, how can anyone make the journey?

This is why the desert fathers and mothers taught that each novice was to have a spiritual guide — someone who knew where the Big Bad Wolves lived as their Little Red Riding Hoods naively walked down the path. Today, we might call these guides "spiritual directors" or "disciplers."

LEADERS AND THE DESERT

For us, enmeshed in our leadership roles, a desert monk may seem as irrelevant as a cactus. We face nagging issues that try our patience and daily we struggle with difficult people and worrisome deadlines.

Yet, the Salts have something to teach us. With their ultimate goal of a quiet trust in God, they encourage us not to be satisfied with a superficial spirituality. They remind us that Christian spirituality is as deep as we want to go.

They also remind us that, as Christian leaders, we also are meant to be Salts. The world around us is as parched as a desert, and we must find new means to be an influence for Christ in our involved situations. In the chapters ahead we will look at specific ways we can do this.

15
Living by Values and Ethics

What a name — Nabal. It means "fool." We encounter his story in I Samuel 25, where we learn that he owned an agri-business consisting of a thousand goats and three thousand sheep. By the way, his family name — Caleb — was no better. It means "dog."

The biblical story tells how David and his men protected "Fool Dog" and his flocks from predatory animals and thieves. When feast time came, David expected a gratuity for his services, but Fool Dog would have none of it. Instead, he gave David a generous insult.

David responded like any Bedouin warrior would. With his honor at stake and consumed by anger, he marches his men to teach Fool Dog a lesson. Along the way, Abigail, Nabal's wife, meets David before the blood flowed.

She admits that her husband is just like his name, a fool, but then she craftily says that whoever murders a fool becomes one in turn. She reminds David of his life's mission –one day he was meant to be king. Does the future king want needless bloodshed on his conscience? Why should David kill others wantonly when God promises to protect him? Abigail appeals to David's spiritual values which he had forgotten in the heat of the conflict.

David's response was to bless her for "good judgment and for keeping me ... from avenging myself" (vs. 33). Yes, it was honorable for him to kill Nabal, but it was neither godly nor wise. Whose values would he live by? What was his real mission anyways? Abigail not only understood who David really was, she also had the courage to tell him of this.

VALUES-BASED DECISION-MAKING

As Christian leaders, we operate in a world filled with our own Fool Dogs and desert conflicts. In the heat of a moment, we may be tempted to forget the values we live by. While ordinary decisions might be done in default mode, that is not good enough for important matters that affect people for a long time. Those decisions have to be done carefully and according to principle. We cannot simply react to situations emotionally with knee-jerk choices.

In the story of David and Abigail, she forced David into what we would call a values-based decision-making process. In it she purposely caused

David to think through his values while he deliberated over Fool Dog's fate.

It is always helpful to have an Abigail or two in any organization. But we can also follow an "Abigail Process."

The Abigail Process begins when an organization clearly understands its own mission and values. This takes time. The development of a clear mission and the delineation of an organization's values involve a process of discussion, feedback, education and vision-casting. The process is well-worth it, though, because once people know who they are, they find it easier to figure out what they want when important decisions have to be made.

Below is a simplified version of a values-based decision-making process:

The 'Abigail' Process

DEFINE

The Abigail process begins when an organization first defines its mission and core values before any specific issue arises.

DISCERN

An issue is presented. The team discerns the values at play behind the issue and compares them with the organization's core values.

CREATE

The team thinks creatively about the options that best support its organizational values in the light of the situation.

IMPLEMENT

The team implements its best option and re-evaluates the situation in due time.

MAKING ETHICAL DECISIONS

We can follow an Abigail Process for heat-of-the-moment decisions. But sometimes we also need to do deeper ethical thinking as leaders.

Since leadership involves the use of power to influence others toward a goal, ethical problems in leadership often arise over how we use our power. Whether we know it or not, our decisions can affect the lives of people unjustly and unfairly.

For instance, an organization in an economic contraction struggles to survive. As a leader, you want to develop a plan that will enable your organization to survive yet be as just as possible to your personnel. You are facing an ethical issue, not because you abused anyone, but because you know that your choices will affect lives.

As Christian leaders, we want to do the right thing, but this can be very difficult to discern at times. People often rely on a single theory of ethics to guide their choices in a situation, but each theory is limited.

Some, for instance, consider the "ethical thing" to be whatever does **the greatest good** for society as a whole. But we do not always know in advance what the greatest good will be in the long run. It is also possible that our sense of the "greatest good" will be horribly warped, as when the Nazis in

World War II thought the greatest good to be the extermination of the Jewish race.

Another approach in ethics has been to do **the most correct thing,** whatever the cost. But ethical dilemmas are shrouded by confusing and conflicting views, making it difficult for us always to know the correct thing to do. Not only that, but we also can have a very twisted sense of what is correct, just as we can have for what is the greatest good.

Some then say that we should do **the most loving thing,** whatever the cost. But, again, people have disagreed about what is the most loving thing to do. Is spanking a child a loving act, or a crime? Is capital punishment beneficial, or barbaric? Is going to war to defend a homeland a loving thing to do? People have their differing views.

Other people base their sense of ethics on **the most just thing** to do. But when this theory is applied to the political realm and economic redistribution is sought, it raises the question whether it penalizes effort and thereby causes society to be *less* productive and just.

Still another ethical approach has been to do **the most responsible thing** for society as a whole. But who determines what is the most responsible behavior in a community?

In many countries, **the most honorable thing** is considered to be the most ethical. Honor can be a great motivator for sacrifice but it, too, can lead to such a bizarre action as a father who kills his daughter for violating the family honor with a young man. The values which determine the most honorable thing vary among cultures.

Many base their sense of ethics on whatever is **the most loyal thing** to do toward a leader or a group. In this situation, truth is determined by what is best for the group. But this can lead to problems such as adopting unquestioning obedience to a leader who does evil.

Still other people base their sense of right and wrong on what is **most profitable** for their lives, or **most pleasurable**, or **the least troublesome**. But these are certainly self-centered notions of ethics.

No matter what approach we use, we quickly realize that there are limitations and that it is not always easy to determine the most ethical thing to do. At best, we can use all the approaches together to think through an issue from different angles in the hope of making the most informed decision.

When a leadership team must make a decision involving a difficult ethical choice, it must understand the issue as broadly as possible. The team members would follow a values-based decision-making approach, but then ask further questions to widen their understanding. They might, for instance, ask:

> Who will be affected negatively by our decision?
>
> Can we foresee any of the long-term consequences?
>
> In this decision, are we simply being loyal to our organization or are we truly making an ethical choice?
>
> Are we able to explain our reasoning and motives to the world?
>
> Will we be comfortable with our decision years from now?
>
> What cultural issues do we need to consider?

A serious problem in leadership teams — one that can undermine ethical decision-making —is "*groupthink.*" This is when the members of a team feel the need to be agreeable toward each other more than to truly resolve a problem. When this happens, everyone tends to adopt a single point of view to be nice to each other or because they feel pressured to agree. Communication breaks down as people hide their real opinions. Facts go unchecked or ignored. The result can be fatal.

Leaders can discourage *groupthink* by encouraging free and open discussions and debate and by soliciting contrary views without penalty. People can be taught to be tough, loyal and respectful of each other.

THE VALUE OF AN ETHICAL STANDARD

Christian leaders foster the ethical climate of an organization not only through the ethical decision process, but also by maintaining ethical standards. When the 20th century Christian leader Billy Graham first came into prominence, he and his team developed an ethical code to follow. It read:

> We will never criticize, condemn, or speak negatively about others.
>
> We will be accountable, particularly in handling finances, with integrity according to the highest business standards.
>
> We will tell the truth and be thoroughly honest, especially in reporting statistics.
>
> We will be exemplary in morals — clear, clean and careful to avoid the very appearance of any impropriety.

Graham's standards set such a tone that they influenced many other Christian leaders as well.

Many businesses and organizations have developed their own ethical codes of conduct, but these codes are only as good as the leaders who enforce them. There is a difference between paper standards and true operating norms. A company that says it does not participate in corruption may quietly do so to keep a contract. It is the leader who must insist on what the ethical standards will be during times of choice.

BRIBERY AND CORRUPTION

It is especially difficult to know what to do when corruption has become systemic. We may begin thinking, "Corruption is the norm. I must fit in with the system." But is our goal just to get things done? Is it not to change the world-system?

Those who live in such cultures are very aware of the harmfulness of bribes and corruption and often wish it could end. They may be surprisingly open to businesses and organizations which adhere to higher standards. In the 1990's and early 2000's, mainland China was switching rapidly from a planned to a market economy. Widespread problems with corruption were reported but there was also openness to learning from companies which followed a higher standard. Christian leaders can lead the way in modeling these standards. Our goal is not simply to get things done, but to get them done in a way that transforms culture.

Still, it takes a great deal of discernment to respond in the right way to situations in which gifts are expected. It is helpful to distinguish between gifts which manipulate and gifts which express gratitude without manipulation. The former corrupts a society, while the later may just help an underpaid worker to survive. And certainly, gifts are never to be received or given to influence a judge in a court of law.

In trying to decide the right thing to do, we can ask ourselves such questions as:

> "If press reporters knew about this gift, would they call it corrupt?"

> "Will the gift compromise my Christian witness in the long-term, even if it gets things done for me in the short-term?"

> "Is this gift being used to influence a verdict or a judge?"

> "Am I using this gift to manipulate, or to express gratitude?"

> "Have I prayed for God to help me in this situation?"

ETHICS IN MULTI-CULTURAL SITUATIONS

The word "culture" refers to the shared history, attitudes, values, perspectives and practices that characterize a people. Because of these differences, conflicts and misunderstandings can easily erupt in multi-cultural settings.

Years ago, I taught a class in an overseas situation. No matter what I said, one individual always opposed me vigorously. At the time, I felt he was just being ill-tempered. Years, however, one of his countrymen spoke candidly to me about the colonialism which left many from their generation feeling inferior around expatriate teachers. He said the oppositional behavior I experienced was due to this.

When a multi-cultural team works through an ethical issue, everyone comes to the table with their own residual backgrounds. The members must learn to talk on a heart-level about their differing values and motives. The team must recognize, for instance, that cultures often have prevailing theories of ethics just as individual people do. One nationality may be very concerned with individual justice and equality, but another nationality might be more concerned with group loyalty. Each culture will have its own sense of right and wrong.

Decision-making on such a team requires a broadening of perspectives until the values of each culture is properly respected. Only then can a decision be achieved that is sensitive to the situation. Decisions based solely on the preferences of one cultural group are counter-productive.

THE ULTIMATE GOAL

We have seen how people tend to base their ethical sense on certain goals they desire to achieve. It could be that they are seeking the greatest good, or the most correct thing to do, or the most loving thing. They could also be seeking to determine what is the most just choice in a situation, or the most responsible, or the most honorable or the most loyal.

Ultimately, from a Christian perspective, our ethical decision-making is a process of trying to determine what is **the most pleasing thing to God**. Only God is completely holy and just and good. Our role is to determine, to the best of our abilities, what is right in God's eyes.

We do this by using the various theories of ethics to examine an issue from different perspectives. But, as Christians, we also have the help of the Holy Spirit. When faced with a difficult ethical decision, many leaders quietly pray for wisdom and discernment. In the next chapter we will learn more about understanding the mind of God in the complicated situations we face.

16

Seeking Wisdom and Guidance

Many who bring faith to leadership want to know if God guides leaders directly. Should we expect God to tell us explicitly what to do in all the critical situations we face as leaders? Would that not be great?

One school of thought says that we should, indeed, expect this to happen. The view assumes that God has a perfect plan for everyone and every group. Our role as leaders is to discover what is next on God's agenda for the people we lead and then to move them on to that agenda. If we receive no specific guidance, then we are to take no new action until we do so.

Another school of thought says that God does *not* have a perfect plan for everyone and every group and therefore does not guarantee us specific guidance. We can pray for providential guidance, and it may come. But if it does not, we are free to make our own choices using our own godly wisdom.

Certainly, God is capable of giving us providential guidance. The question here is whether we always should expect this to happen. We need to ask, "Does God have a perfect plan for each of our lives and organizations?"

DOES GOD HAVE A PERFECT PLAN FOR US?

Let's assume, for the sake of argument, that God does, indeed, have a detailed blueprint for each of our lives. What are the implications?

Let's say that I have married a woman named Jeanne, but it wasn't in God's perfect plan for me to do so. Maybe it was God's perfect plan for me to marry Mei, yet I did not. Logically, that means I am now out of God's perfect plan for my life and Jeanne is my second-best wife. God might bless our marriage, but not as much as if I had I married Mei, as God really had intended.

Let's also say that, according to God's perfect plan, I was supposed to meet Mei the day after I married Jeanne. We never met as God intended because Jeanne and I were on our honeymoon. Mei is now not in God's perfect will, even though she never even met me. It does not really matter — she still is not in God's perfect will. Poor Mei.

Mei ended up marrying Tomas. That means both of them are now not in God's perfect plan because Mei was supposed to marry me. If Tomas marries

Mei, then he is not able to marry the person he was supposed to marry according to "The Plan." Through no fault of their own, they're all out of God's perfect plan — all because of me!

And it just goes on like that. Because I did not marry Mei as God intended, then the entire human race will eventually fall out of God's perfect plan. One little mistake and I have destroyed humanity.

It appears that God does not have a rigid, perfect plan for each of us. When we say that there is a detailed life-plan for each of our lives, we actually are believing in fatalism. And we are saying that we have a deterministic God.

God is not like that. And this is why the Bible never promises us that we can have specific guidance from God on demand. We experience God's providential care every day. And we also may receive direct guidance on occasion, but this does not imply this must always happen.

GOD'S MASTER PLAN

The Bible never teaches that there is a detailed blueprint for each of our lives, but it does teach that God has a Master Plan for the salvation of the world, a plan that culminates in Christ (Ephesians 3:7-11). When we come to Christ, we become a part of this Master Plan. We may even experience

God's providential guidance according to the purposes of this Master Plan.

Other than that, we should recognize that God's providential care for us also allows us to have considerable freedom in the choices we make. It is this way because God wants us to be mature and responsible. We are made in the image of God and have been endowed by our Creator with considerable freedom. Our lives with God are travel adventures in which we actually get to make many of the choices on the trip.

So, when Paul talks about a woman seeking marriage, he writes: "She is free to marry anyone she wishes, but he must belong to the Lord" (I Corinthians 7:39). The choice is entirely her's, so long as she chooses a believer. If she is free to choose which believer to marry — a most important decision — then certainly we also must be free to make many of our choices in life, as long as we conform to God's moral will. If God wishes to redirect us in our choice, he is capable of doing so.

THE LEADING OF THE SPIRIT

What about the leading of the Spirit?

In the Scriptures we read how the Spirit provides specific guidance and even geographical leading. Luke 4:1 tells us that Jesus "was led by the Spirit in the desert." Similarly, Acts 8:39 tells us how the "Spirit of the Lord suddenly took Philip away," and Acts 16:7 mentions that the "Spirit of Jesus would not allow" Paul and his companions to enter Bithynia. This specific guidance happened at God's initiative and to fulfill God's Master Plan. Such guidance is possible, but we cannot always expect to receive it.

Two major passages concerning the leading of the Spirit are Romans 8 and Galatians 5. There, the context relates the leading of the Spirit to our daily walk, or behavior, and not to specific guidance. The Spirit leads us to live a godly life by convicting us and compelling us to develop the fruit of the Spirit: love, joy, peace, patience, kindness, goodness, faithfulness, gentleness and self-control (Galatians 5:18-25).

Some say that certain Psalms suggest we can expect to receive specific guidance through leading:

> Show me your ways, O Lord, teach me your paths; guide me in your truth and teach me. ... He guides the humble in what is right and teaches them his way. (Psalm 25:4, 9)

> I will instruct you and teach you in the way you should go; I will counsel you and watch over you. (Psalm 32:8)

But in these verses, "ways" and "paths" are metaphors for the demands of God's covenant as found in the Law of Moses (see Psalm 25:10, Deuteronomy 8:6). The verses are not promising that God will supernaturally tell us what to do; they are promising that God guides us as we study God's ways in God's word.

Some also refer to John 14:26. It reminds us that the Spirit "will teach you all things and will remind you of everything I have said to you." But this is not a promise of guidance, only that the Spirit would help the Apostles to recall Jesus' teachings and its significance.

So, the biblical evidence is that we may experience the specific guidance of the Spirit, but no verse promises this to us on demand. We should certainly pray for providential guidance, but if an answer does not come within a reasonable time, we should assume that God has given the matter over to us to decide. The evidence of the scriptures is that God also can work through our decisions based on godly wisdom.

MAKING WISE AND GODLY DECISIONS

The biblical understanding of guidance contrasts noticeably with that of the pagan nations in ancient history. The records of ancient Assyria and Babylon are filled with accounts of divination — attempts to obtain specific guidance from the gods through such methods as examining the quivering of a freshly-killed liver. But there is a world of difference between examining a liver in a bowl and reading the scriptures. The study of God's ways and character in the scriptures helped the Hebrew people to make wise and godly decisions.

The Scriptures teach us such basic things as to tell the truth, to respect property rights and to honor marriage. The Law also teaches us principles of justice such as:

- punishment should not be excessive
- land inheritance is to be secure
- the poor are not to be oppressed
- respect is to be shown to foreigners
- no one is above the law, not even the king
- compassion is to be shown to animals
- all in society are to rest regularly

Furthermore, the scriptures teach us about God's character. When we learn what God is like, we learn what pleases him. In Exodus 34:6-7, for instance, we learn that God is "compassionate and gracious." This teaches us to act in a similar way toward others.

The prophets teach us to be just, like God is just:

And what does the LORD require of you? To act justly and to love mercy and to walk humbly with your God. (Micah 6:8)

But let justice roll on like a river, righteousness like a never-failing stream! (Amos 5:24)

> Is not this the kind of fasting I have chosen: to loose the chains of injustice and untie the cords of the yoke, to set the oppressed free and break every yoke? Is it not to share your food with the hungry and to provide the poor wanderer with shelter - when you see the naked, to clothe him, and not to turn away from your own flesh and blood? (Is. 58:6-7)

The Bible is not a comprehensive casebook which details what we are to do in every situation. Instead, it teaches us what God is like so we can decide what pleases God the most. When we read about God's words and ways, we gain insight into God's will in the various situations we face. We grow in godly wisdom.

ACTIVE AND PASSIVE DISCIPLES

When we think that God has a detailed blueprint for each of our lives, it promotes passivity since we are not supposed to make any major decision until we hear a word from God. This passivity may explain why some leaders never develop their fullest potential. They let too many choices and opportunities slip away. We can be like the man in Jesus' parable who buries his master's money instead of investing it.

Years ago, an international leader asked me, "Should I wait on God to show me what to do next, or should I go ahead and make my wisest choice?" He was a godly man who relied on prayer, but he was wondering about specific guidance.

We talked about Ecclesiastes 9:10, which says, "Whatever your hand finds to do, do it with all your might." And we also talked about Philippians 2:12 that reads, "Continue to work out your salvation with fear and trembling, for it is God who works in you to will and to act according to his good purpose."

I told him, "Make your wisest choice and trust God to honor it and work through it. You're a godly man. Pray and ask for help, then act boldly." After that, my friend started a home for disadvantaged children in an impoverished country. He received no specific guidance to do so – he just did it. And God blessed his decision. My friend also became involved in Christian media work. He received no specific guidance to do so – he just did it to honor God. And God has blessed that work as well.

The biblical teaching is that we should be pro-active and bold as disciples since we are responsible to God for our lives. When making decisions, we should rely both on prayer for discernment as well as on godly wisdom.

17
Keeping Integrity

After reviewing the 150 leadership studies mentioned in chapter one, Laura Reave concluded that *personal integrity* is "the most important element for engendering follower respect and trust."

Integrity is absolutely necessary to authentic leadership. Whenever we seek to lead others in a spiritual way, we will be tempted to compromise ourselves. The demonic will seek to render us ineffective by distorting our motives and values.

Just before Jesus became a national leader, the demonic tempted Jesus in the desert to compromise his integrity (Matthew 4:1-11). Would he emerge from the desert true to himself and his Father, or not? The three trials of integrity he faced are common to all leaders. They are the trials of despair, pride and ruthlessness.

THE TRIAL OF DESPAIR
In the desert, the Spirit of God led Jesus to hunger. Earlier, when the Israelites hungered in the

desert, they despaired and demanded food from God. But Jesus just quietly trusted in his Father. He affirms, "Man does not live on bread alone but on every word that comes from the mouth of the Lord" (Deuteronomy 8:3).

In our leadership, there may be times when we are tempted to despair. God may allow us to experience situations beyond our ability to cope. While it is generally unwise for us to work beyond our limits, sometimes we know we must do so to fulfill God's will.

Robert Wilder felt that way in 1886. He was one of a hundred students who sensed the time was ripe to create a student movement to bring Christ to the world. Wilder was chosen to share this vision in the universities of America, but his health was precarious and he suffered a total collapse after the first meetings.

Risking a permanent breakdown, Wilder continued with his meetings anyways and trusted God to help. Over the next eight months, he visited a hundred sixty-two institutions and motivated over two thousand people to service. He created a student movement which became a major factor in introducing the Gospel to Korea, China and India — yet none of it would have happened if Wilder had given up in despair.

Sometimes, we are called to go beyond our limits in order to do what we know to be right. Just as Christ maintained his integrity by trusting God in the face of despair, so must we.

THE TRIAL OF PRIDE

In his second attempt to destroy Jesus' integrity as a leader, Satan told Jesus to jump off the Temple in Jerusalem. He even quoted Psalm 91 to ensure his safety. Not even "your foot will suffer harm," he quoted, as if the Psalm were an insurance policy that guaranteed angelic protection.

If Jesus harbored a drop of pride in his heart, he would have jumped. After all, what an amazing miracle it would have been! But Jesus refused to do so because he loved his Father. The miracles would come later, but always at his Father's bidding and for his Father's purpose.

From the desert fathers comes the story of a miracle-worker who decided he would go to Rome and convert the city through wonders. In the end, he chose to remain in the desert because he knew it all came from his pride. Had he gone to Rome, he would have lost God. That's why Jesus remained in the desert instead of jumping off the Temple in Jerusalem. And that is why many of the best leaders just quietly continue to serve in obscure places. To stay true.

What does this say to us as leaders?

Sometimes, the life of a leader is as dull as forty days in a desert. Endless meetings and duties can make us feel that we are masters of the monotonous, boldly going nowhere. When we lack recognition, our wounded pride makes us want life to be more interesting and fulfilling. That's when Satan dangles before us a fancy to jump into.

It could be a vast project that we dream up to make us feel worthy, or an illicit affair to be excited over. The second temptation reminds us that ego-feeding can lead us far astray from God.

The typical church scandal involving a male pastor and a female parishioner begins with the unmet needs of both. Often, the woman had an aloof father. As she experiences the warmth and compassion of her pastor, she regards him as an ideal male and begins to adore him. In return, he is attracted to her because she fulfills a need in his life to be appreciated. Since the affair meets subterranean needs in both lives, they can rationalize it to the point of seeing nothing wrong with it. But in so doing, they will have jumped off a cliff.

THE TRIAL OF RUTHLESSNESS
In his third attempt on Jesus' integrity, Satan spits out, "Worship me and I'll give you the world!"

Well, the world is not his to give, but Satan always seems to convince us otherwise.

Behind this temptation is the ancient Middle Eastern notion that gods controlled locales. If you want to prosper, worship the local god. That's why, when Israel entered Canaan, God warned them not to worship the Canaanite gods (Deuteronomy 6:14). Seen in this light, Satan's claim seems clownish: he thinks he is the power-broker for the entire world! Yet, his temptation had a purpose. He was trying to get Jesus to turn ruthless and become like the leaders of the world — to become a Caesar.

In our leadership, we also have to decide if we will emulate the servanthood of Christ or the ruthlessness of Caesar.

In his *Gallic Wars*, Caesar boasts how he slaughtered a million Gauls. He never mentions how his campaign was entirely needless — something he fostered just to win glory for himself. Yet, Caesar and his imitators — the strong, ruthless types — always seem to appeal to us as leaders. Deep down inside, we wonder if they actually do make the better leaders.

Caesar's style of leadership became the prevailing model in the Roman world and even permeated the church. Paul writes of evangelists who preached out of "selfish ambition." He groans, "everyone looks out for his own interests, not those of Jesus Christ." Of Timothy, a true servant-leader, Paul admits, "I have no one else like him" (Philippians 1:17, 2:20-21). Back then, most of the Christians had Caesar in their blood.

Paul vividly contrasts Christ's leadership with that of Caesar's:

> Your attitude should be the same as that of Christ Jesus:
> Who, being in very nature God,
> did not consider equality with God something to be grasped,
> but made himself nothing, taking the very nature of a servant,
> being made in human likeness.
> And being found in appearance as a man,
> he humbled himself and became obedient to death—
> even death on a cross!
> Therefore God exalted him to the highest place
> and gave him the name that is above every name ...
> (Philippians 2:5-11)

In Caesar's world, *humility* was a derogatory word reserved for slaves. In Christ's world, humility is a virtue. Paul recasts the meaning of greatness for us. It's down, then up. Serving, then glory. Christ is our example. Humility is our virtue, not Caesar's arrogant pride.

CONCLUSION

Satan sought to destroy Jesus' integrity with the trials of despair, pride and ruthlessness. If Satan had succeeded in any of these attempts, Jesus would have lost his integrity as a leader.

When we desire to lead others in a spiritual way, the demonic also will tempt us to compromise ourselves. The exact trial will be as varied as the human experience, but it usually will reflect the same old themes of despair, pride and ruthlessness. Satan appeals to our shadow side to make us go berserk with fear and desperation.

Jesus' response always was to remember that he had a Father in heaven who was sufficient for him. His strong trust in God's providential care kept him from losing his integrity in the face of trial.

In the next chapter we will learn more about how we can develop a similar trust in Providence.

18

Finding Serenity

A lake of ink must have been consumed with all that has been written about stress management over the years. Yet, Christian spirituality still offers additional help for leaders under stress besides the typical breathing exercises and relaxation techniques so commonly taught.

We believe in something called Holy Serenity. It is the assurance that no matter what happens to us in this world, we are safe and we have a future with God. Holy Serenity differs from happiness, so focused on outward circumstances. Holy Serenity is the peace that comes to us no matter what our outward circumstances may be.

How do we cultivate Holy Serenity? We do so by renewing our sense of the providence of God in our lives.

OUR BABYLONS

In the Bible, we read of King Nebuchadnezzar strolling about his royal palace. Stretching before his eyes lay Babylon, his greatest achievement. He remarks, "Is not this the great Babylon I have built by my mighty power?" (Daniel 4:30). Immediately, a voice from heaven interrupts to inform him otherwise: "Your royal authority has been taken from you."

Leaders are the doers and shapers of the world. Because we are such causative agents, the temptation is to think that everything happens because of us. Like Nebuchadnezzar, we easily can forget about God's providential working in the world.

As a young pastoral leader, I was like that. I believed in God but found it hard to trust in God to act. I thought it all depended on me. It took five years of head-banging before I learned to just relax and work more in harmony with what the Spirit of God was doing.

Whatever our Babylon may be, whether a church or an organization or an entire city, we have to learn to let God help us. As Christian leaders, we are agents for God in our spheres of influence. We should expect God to give us providential wisdom in the situations we face.

Providence has been called the "forgotten teaching" of Christianity. Indeed, in some parts of the world, it has become virtually abandoned with the rise of secularism. Yet, Jesus clearly taught about providence in such words as:

> Seek first his kingdom and his righteousness, and all these things will be given to you as well. Therefore do not worry about tomorrow, for tomorrow will worry about itself. Each day has enough trouble of its own. (Matthew 6:33-34)

In this teaching, Jesus is telling us that there are two ways we can view life: either by recognizing signs of our heavenly Father at work everywhere, or not.

When we see our Lord watching over his creation — nurturing it, providing for it and caring for it, it affects how we live: we find ourselves trusting in our heavenly Father. But when we think there is no heavenly Father, we are left with just a cold, harsh world. We have no one to turn to in our times of need. We sense no caring presence. Instead, we begin worrying about everything, because we're all alone.

In Matthew 6, Jesus contrasts these two ways of looking at the world and he tries to jolt us out of the one and into the other. He tells us plainly, "Do not worry about your life." It's a command he's giving us to stop worrying.

We all worry. If we're supposed to be at a meeting at 8:00 am, we can't saunter in at 10:00 am and say, "I don't worry." At that point, maybe we should. But Jesus is not talking about life's exigencies. The Greek word here is *merimnao*. It refers to obsessive worry — when our minds become filled with so much anxiety and paralyzing fear that we can no longer sense God's care.

In place of this obsessive worry, Jesus tells us to dwell our thoughts on the goodness of our Father. "Consider the birds of the air," Jesus said. "They neither sow nor reap nor store away in barns, and yet your heavenly Father feeds them. Are you not much more valuable than they?" Everyday, God showers his goodness on the birds. If they recognize it, should not we?

THE PROBLEM OF SUFFERING

Many people have abandoned a belief in providence because they cannot get beyond the problem of suffering. They ask, "How could a good God allow suffering?" Perhaps they knew someone they loved dearly who suffered terribly and the emotional trama remains within them.

When I think about that question, my mind goes back to a man whose wife had died from cancer. He himself had just learned he also had cancer and was dying from it, but I noticed he was calm and at peace. I asked him, "Where does your peace come from?"

In reply, he told me a story.

"One evening when my wife was alive, but sick with her cancer," he said, "she suddenly turned to me and asked me, 'Do you see him?'"

"See who?" he replied.

"The angel. There's an angel standing at the foot of our bed and he's looking at us."

Now, this man carefully explained to me that his wife was not on medication at the time. Nor was she half asleep. She just suddenly saw an angel.

"Is he telling you anything?" he asked her.

"No, he's just there, not saying anything, but I feel a deep peace."

The vision lasted for only a few moments and then ended — but from that time on, she lived with a peace that never left her and continued on in him. God cured neither of them from their cancers, but instead he gave them something else to live by — hope.

We do not know why bad things happen, but God's goodness is still everywhere around us. It's in the beauty of the sky, in the kindness of people, in miracles. We see it in the sun shining, the wind blowing and our hearts beating. Jesus reminds us of the birds, how they experience God's goodness every day. God is so good, Jesus says, that "He causes his sun to rise on the evil and the good" (Matthew 5:45).

Jesus wants us to sense the goodness of God all about us. He wants us to get our eyes off our worries and our troubles and experience all of God's care and grace that he has for us ... if we but have the eyes to see.

YOU MICRO-FAITHS!

Two ways of viewing life - under God's providential care, or not. Which way describes us as leaders? If we're honest, we'll all probably say, "I'm somewhere in the middle. I believe in God, but I often feel anxious."

When we are like this, Jesus has a word for us. He calls us "you-who-are-of-little-faith" (Matthew 6:30). It's all one word in the Greek, and can be translated something like "You micro-faiths!" When we do not trust in God's providential care like Jesus expects us to, we are micro-faith believers.

He told the people of his time not to worry obsessively whether or not they will have enough food or water or clothing. Lacking provisions like that would make us very worried. Yet, even then, Jesus counseled them not to allow themselves to become consumed by worry. If that is how Jesus spoke to them, what would he say to us who have so much?

Sometimes, God has to teach us the hard way to develop this kind of trust in providence. Sometimes, we are taken through desperate moments to learn. In one desperate time in my life, I experienced an instantaneous healing. When it happened, I heard the Voice speak to my heart: "If your very health depends on Me, so does your life and work." It taught me deeply about providence.

EXPERIENCING GOD DAILY

Living under providence is nothing less than enjoying a relationship with the living God. The Lord wants us to share our worries and concerns with him.

Years ago, I taught some young adults about providence. I challenged them, "Allow yourself to experience God … in the morning, talk to God about whatever worried you for that day. Just tell him what you are facing. Is it a difficult person you have to deal with? Do you need wisdom to face a situation? Are you under pressure? Whatever it is, talk to God about it. Ask for God's help, give it into God's hands and then see how God helps you through the day."

Most of them just scoffed at the idea, but one young woman accepted the challenge. The next week, she came back with a big smile on her face and said, "It works! I felt like God was helping me all day long! I couldn't believe it."

A few years later I saw her again after she went off to university. The first thing she told me was,

"I'm still doing what you taught me and it's totally changed my life. I'm continuing to experience God every day."

One spiritual discipline that helps us build an awareness of providence is called the "prayer of examen," a spot check that keeps our hearts responsive to God's care.

In it, we pause and review what has been happening in our day. We try to recognize God's gifts of love for us — things that may be as simple as the smile of a friend that we enjoyed. We also review our motives and actions, whether or not we responded to God like we should have, or remained dull of heart. We end by talking to the Lord honestly about what we need to do to be more in tune with him.

The providence of God is not an abstract theological concept but something we are meant to live by every day. When we learn to trust in God's providential workings, it calms our fears and worries, it helps our prayers to be less demanding and impetuous, and it creates in us the knowledge that — despite whatever may happen to us in this world — we are safe. As leaders, our trust in God's providence can help us in the organizations we lead.

19

Walking Humbly

They were called Sophists — the "Wise Ones." They were wandering philosophers who gave public lectures throughout ancient Greece. Since the traditional religious cults of Greece concerned themselves only with ritual and never with ethics or morality, the Sophists filled the void. They taught the people how to live life. The common people came in hordes and gladly paid money to hear what these learned men had to say.

The Sophists were also excellent orators. Ever since the time of Aristotle, Greeks treated their orators like pop stars. The people loved to listen to the Sophists with their dazzling, oratorical techniques. Since the Sophists were also very impressive in demeanor, taking care to look the part of erudite professors, they provided a compelling model to the Greeks for what a leader was supposed to be like.

Compared to the Sophists, Paul was a disturbing contrast. His critics pointed out that he was physically unimpressive and a drip of a speaker.

"His bodily presence is weak and his speech of no account," they remarked (2 Corinthians 10:9-10). They called Paul's speaking ability "amateurish" because he did not use oratorical tricks to manipulate his audiences (2 Corinthians 11:6).

However, Paul had something which the Sophists lacked: a heart for God. This made him able to sense the human pride behind Sophism, with its focus on external appearances and fame and manipulation. The Gospel was fundamentally different from this.

The Christians in Corinth became enamored by the Sophic model of leadership. When they did so, they lost their hearts for God. They wanted only leaders who were impressive in demeanor and sophisticated in speech (1 Corinthians 1:18-25).

Their pride-centered spirituality gave rise to a host of problems: personality cults, sexual immorality, lawsuits and gross insensitivity. Time and again in his letters, Paul calls the Corinthians back to the cross. He urges them to "imitate me" (1 Corinthians 4:16). Sophic leadership may look and sound impressive, but it is not the same as godly leadership.

SOPHISM TODAY

The Sophists were the professional leaders of their day. In contrast to them, Paul looked like an amateur. Although he possessed spiritual authority — something that the Sophists lacked — Paul did not measure up to the reigning model of what it meant to be a professional.

Immediately, this raises the question in our minds, "How might professional leaders today resemble the ancient Sophic leaders?"

The answer is evident: at the heart of the Sophic model of leadership lay a deep-seated pride. The wandering lecturers made themselves look impressive and sound convincing to acquire power. Today, when our pride motivates us to gain power over others, we are being exactly like the Sophists.

Pride is the desire to be above another person to give ourselves a sense of meaning. Pride comes with a price. St. John Cassian wrote, "Pride corrupts the whole soul, not just part of it." [1] It does this by deluding us and filling us with a sense of self-importance and making us incapable of recognizing the value of others. C. S. Lewis wrote in *Mere Christianity* that it "eats up the very possibility of love, or contentment, or even common sense."

Pride makes us always to want to be on top. It can lead us into such aberrant practices of

---

1 St. John Cassian, On the Eight Vices: On Pride.

dominance such as only listening to ourselves, or constantly putting other people down, or conquering other people sexually, or seeking an exorbitant salary.

For many highly-motivated leaders, pride can become their chronic sin. Charles Colson, who was jailed for the infamous Nixon scandal of the 1970's, spoke repeatedly about the culture of pride that deludes high leaders. Although he once vowed never to be unethical, he admitted in 2008, "I now realize that every human being has an infinite capacity for self-rationalization and self-delusion."

In the sight of God, all our human pride is nothing less than boasting. That's why Jesus says that the kingdom belongs to the "poor in spirit" (Matthew 5:3). He tells the story about a tax collector who beats his chest and utters, "God, have mercy on me, a sinner" (Luke 18:9-14). And Paul writes how grace is "not by works so that no one can boast" (Ephesians 2:9).

From a Christian perspective, the object of life is not dominance, but the maturing of the human soul. This begins when our hearts become broken before God. It is only then that we discover grace.

POWER AND AUTHORITY

When we find grace and its accompanying virtue of humility, it changes our concept of power. It teaches us the difference between having power and achieving authority.

As leaders, we know how power works and how to use it — that's how we got to be leaders in the first place. Because we know power, it is easy for us to think of leadership in terms of dominance, self-importance or self-fulfillment.

But when base our lives on God's grace, all of this changes. We begin to realize that our true security lies in God alone. This frees us from joining in the naked pursuit for power that consumes the lives of so many professional leaders. We begin to understand that the goal of Christian leadership is to serve God, not to be dominant. This causes us to achieve authority.

Jesus' decision to die on the Cross was a horrible career move. If he acted like professionals do today, he would have avoided it at all costs. Yet, the cross proved to be the crux of history because Jesus knew the difference between power and authority.

How do we apply this to leadership?

When Boeing designed the 777 jetliner, the company wanted to build the safest plane in the world. To reach that goal, they made a fundamental change in their management style by cultivating organizational humility. The management decided to listen to anyone who felt there was a problem — even to low-ranking people.

Reportedly, there was opposition to this. Before, when an engineer encountered a problem, he or she would try to solve it alone. But in forcing everyone to be open about their difficulties, management created an atmosphere that solved problems quicker than before.

Contrast this with the maiden voyage of the Titanic in 1912. Captain Edward John Smith insisted on racing the vessel at top speed even though icebergs were reported nearby. He wanted to impress the world with the speed of the Titanic's maiden voyage across the icy North Atlantic.

Humility caused the 777 jetliner to become a safe aircraft. Pride sank the Titanic. Might we say that humility works better?

Authority only grows when there is humility.

20
Seeking the Good of Others

One day, I was talking with several students from an urban class I was teaching. Across from me sat Luis, a Latino man in his thirties, and Ephraim, an older African-American leader. Luis couldn't contain his excitement. He said, "I'm learning so much from this class. I'm telling everyone about it!"

It's great having a student like him around.

But then he added, "When I started telling people about what I am learning, they kept on telling me to keep quiet ... they said, 'others have never had the chance to be in school like you.'"

Luis looked puzzled as we all sat there. Then he said, "I still don't understand it. Aren't we supposed to be getting an education and getting ahead?"

That's when Ephraim, older and wiser, spoke. His words were unforgettable: "I've seen this time and again," he intoned. "Whenever someone gets ahead a little, others are not happy about it. Instead, they accuse you of being better than them.

Whenever you begin succeeding, there are all these hands trying to pull you back down. But we have to learn to help each other succeed instead."

As we sat there, I realized we were talking about the effects of envy, which makes us jealous over another's success and desirous for their failure instead of their good.

The ancient Greeks personified Envy as a woman holding a handful of live, squirming snakes and eating them at the same time! It's a bitter image totally lacking in grace and kindness and full of harshness and destruction.

Envy is a personal sin with clear, cultural effects. A school teacher, a leader in her own right, once told me, "I have plenty of smart students in my class but teaching them is so frustrating. As soon as my students reach a low-average grade, they stop studying. It's an unwritten rule among them that no one is supposed to get ahead. They're afraid of what the others will say." She was describing the effects of envy within her school's culture.

Envy permeates some cultures to such an extent that special amulets are used in attempts to ward off its effects. Belief in the "evil eye," considered to be an envious look that brings destruction, is common in the Middle East, South Asia, Central Asia, West Africa and Mediterranean Europe. In

Islamic cultures, the hand of Fatima is used as a talisman to ward off the evil eye.

ENVY AND LEADERS

Envy affects leaders just as much as anyone. In writing about the problems within corporate leadership, Lee Iacocca, an automotive executive, said in his book, *Where Have All the Leaders Gone?* - "Sometimes I think the real culprit is envy." Executives often measure their worth by their salary, causing compensations to spiral out of sight. The same dynamic is at play even among religious leaders, who often measure their worth by the size of their ministry or their influence among others.

Envy is the sin of comparison. Every time we think we have not succeeded — failure being whatever we think it is — we envy those who appear to have done better.

Envy certainly affects the internal interaction of an organization. A successful team leader, for instance, could evoke the envy of others who will then spread gossip to undermine that leader. Sometimes leaders are not even fully aware of their own envy. Instead, they consign their feelings to the unconscious, and this creates a culture of hidden subterfuges in an organization. Self interest becomes more important than the common good.

THE ANTIDOTE TO ENVY

Christian spirituality offers several strategies to cope with envy. The first is to base our own sense of worth on God instead of others. God loves us. Christ died for us. We are being called to a glorious existence. These may seem like basic thoughts, but when we remind ourselves of them, they give us a sense of our self worth before God.

From a Christian perspective, we also need to remember that leadership is a spiritual gifting and a calling which we receive from God to serve. When we remind ourselves of the nature of our calling from God to be leaders, it keeps us from comparing ourselves to others or turning leadership into a competition.

Several of the spiritual disciplines are especially helpful for dealing with envy. Since envy is the failure to seek the good of another, we can personally adopt those spiritual disciplines which best counteract this.

One such spiritual discipline is that of mentoring, which we have already mentioned. When we mentor, we selflessly develop the potential of other people. Instead of comparing ourselves with others, we are using our skills and knowledge to help others succeed.

Another spiritual discipline that thwarts envy is to be a part of a meaningful Christian fellowship.

There, we learn that we are valued as a part of the whole, but we are not the whole. The Spirit bestows on each person a unique spiritual gift which we use for the common good. When we see a friend being used by God, it becomes an occasion to thank God rather than to feel envious. Paul and Peter could have been natural rivals. Instead, it says that they "recognized the grace" within each other (Galatians 2:7-9).

We also can adopt such a spiritual discipline as deliberately praying for the welfare of those we envy. Or, we can practice the discipline of serving others, such as by volunteering in a project to aid the poor. If we belong to a covenant group, we may wish to share our struggles over envy with others for the purposes of accountability and prayer. All of these disciplines help us to overcome envy by seeking the good of others.

21
Making Peace

An important skill in leadership is the ability to resolve a conflict. For Christians in leadership, we are called to peace-making since Jesus said, "Blessed are the peacemakers." This is not an option, but an essential part of who we are.

It may be our calling, but conflict is often our companion. Since our task as leaders is to move people toward objectives, we frequently have to deal with intransigent organizational attitudes and competing interests among the people we lead. Sometimes, conflict even hardens like concrete in an organization, turning into systemic anger. We may face a whole culture of conflict — marked by hostility, subversion, manipulation, secretiveness, and lingering emotions. All of this can leave us feeling frustrated, annoyed and angry ourselves.

While much is available elsewhere about conflict management, Christian spirituality goes further. It deals with the state of heart that enables us to become peace-makers. Before we can create a culture of peace among the people we lead, we first must understand how to deal with the anger within our own lives.

IS ANGER A SIN?

Many Christian leaders struggle when they feel anger since we have been taught for centuries that anger is a sin. But when we read the Bible we find a more nuanced story.

The most common Hebrew word for anger in the Bible is *aph*. It is used to mean both "nose" and "anger" — since we breathe hard when we get angry! Picture an enraged horse with flared nostrils. The Bible vividly draws upon this image to describe God's anger in 2 Samuel 9, talking about the foundations of the earth being laid bare at the blast from his nostrils. It's God's snorting away in anger.

The Bible is full of similar verses, such as Lamentations 2:3 mentioning the "fierce anger" of God and Jeremiah 7:20 — "My anger ... will be poured out." But such verses make us wonder: if anger is a sin, as we have been told, how could God be angry?

There is also the anger of Jesus to bear in mind. In Mark 3:1-5, Jesus heals a man on the Sabbath, prompting some to condemn him for healing on that day. Mark records how Jesus "looked around at them in anger" for their callousness. In a similar way, in John 2:13-16, Jesus makes a whip and drives out the money changers in high emotion. In Matthew 23, he verbally assails the hypocrisy of the Pharisees. And in Mark 10:13-14, Jesus "was indignant" when his disciples tried to prevent children from coming to him (Mark 10:13-14).

In the Bible, both the God of Israel and Jesus openly display anger. We can only conclude that anger itself is not a sin but an emotion, pure and raw, that comes when something is wrong. That's why the ancient Hebrews could think of God snorting away at evil.

The Bible is an earthy, emotional book. But there are always those for whom it seems too much so. Among the upper classes in ancient Roman society, the philosophy of choice was Stoicism — a reasoned, unemotional way of life. For the Stoics, anger most definitely was a sin. And it also was so among the Greek Platonists, who taught that the divine lacked passion. Both Stoicism and Platonism gave no place for the biblical displays of divine anger.

The Stoic and Platonic bias against anger eventually seeped into Christianity, quietly censoring the biblical portrayals of divine anger in Christian thinking. Despite the Bible's vivid Hebraic descriptions of God in anger, Christian teachers like Augustine and John Cassian taught that God cannot possibly display emotion and that anger is a sin — an idea that continues to the present day.

Yet, despite this, the biblical evidence is plainly there: anger itself is not a sin — it's an emotional response to something that is wrong. The sin lies in the wrong motives we may have behind our anger and in the destructive behavior which may result from it.

DEALING WITH OUR ANGER

When we are angry, the main counsel of the scriptures is to watch our motives and to keep our anger from becoming destructive. Although anger is an emotion, it is invariably impure, especially our quick anger.

We watch our anger by being emotionally honest with ourselves. Paul writes, "'Be angry, but do not sin': Do not let the sun go down while you are still angry" (Ephesians 4:26). It's only when we are first honest with our anger that we can prevent it from curdling into something destructive. Jesus even goes so far as to teach that reconciliation is more important than worship itself (Matthew 5:23-24).

We must be especially careful to become angry only for the right reason. In the Bible, God's anger is never vindictive, but always redemptive. Even when God allows the Babylonians to attack Jerusalem, it is to correct her injustice. And when

Jesus riots against the money changers, it is not a temper-tantrum but a purposeful lesson.

The scriptures counsel us to get angry slowly since this gives us time to reflect and to develop the right motives behind our anger, which often arises from our selfishness, pride, or immaturity. Such anger does not bring about the "righteous life that God desires" (James 1:20, 3:14-16). We read verses such as: "A person with a quick temper does foolish things" (Proverbs 14:17) and "Love ... is not easily angered" (1 Corinthians 13:5). God also is said to be slow to anger (Exodus 34:6).

The cross of Christ also helps us to manage our anger. When we imagine ourselves before the cross and hearing Christ pray for his tormentors, it restrains us. How can we hate a person for whom Christ died, or withhold forgiveness when Jesus prayed for his enemies? Our goal is not to be right; it is to bring all people to salvation. The cross turns us into peace-makers.

MANAGING ANGER IN OTHERS

Once we understand how to deal with our own anger, we become better able to manage it among those we lead. Our goal is not to suppress anger in others, but to keep it from becoming destructive.

When people are in conflict, they often feel powerless, hopeless, confused, fearful and anxious.

An insecure leader will merely react to these raw emotions and never listen to the real issues. Deep inside, people in conflict want to be listened to and respected. They are seeking clear and accurate answers to their questions, Many even wish there could be a win-win outcome and a healing of relationships.

So, our initial goal in a conflict is to move the situation from reaction to conversation. As leaders, we set the tone — by showing respect, by making people feel safe and by listening.

Every leader should acquire the skill of empathetic listening. When we listen empathetically, we are tuning in actively and non-judgmentally to another person. We are allowing them to do the talking. We are showing them genuine interest and trying to bring them out. The psychiatrist and author M. Scott Peck once said, "You cannot truly listen to anyone and do anything else at the same time."

When we do listen well, it builds trust and reduces tension and enables people to work together to solve problems. It shifts the focus in the conflict from reacting to responding.

As Christians, prayer also gives us the strength to respond rather than to react. When we are in a conflict, it is easy to regard people as being 'trouble-makers' or 'obstacles.' Jesus commanded us to pray for our enemies because prayer softens our hearts toward our opponents and connects us with them.

PEACEMAKING AND THE BEATITUDES

The Beatitudes of Jesus embody in words what Jesus did on the cross. On the cross, he overcame evil; in the Beatitudes, he teaches us how to transform evil situations. The Beatitudes are important for Christian leaders because they show us how to defuse tense situations.

The Beatitudes were originally given to disciples on the verge of persecution. Jesus warns them that they would be broken in spirit, would weep, and become marginalized in their own society They would long for justice to come to them (Matthew 5:3-6). Yet, despite all this, Jesus also reminds them that they still have God. Regardless of what they faced, they always would have this assurance.

I am thinking of an African-American woman in my city who experienced a blatant act prejudice against her — one in a never-ending stream. At the end of that difficult day, she came to a prayer meeting in her church. As she knelt by her chair to pray, she wept ceaselessly and clutched her chair tightly and would not let go.

"Lord, give me the strength to forgive one more time," she called out over and over, as the brothers and sisters surrounded her in support. She was living in the spirit of the Beatitudes, trying to draw strength from God in an unjust and harsh world.

The first Beatitudes (5:3-6) teaches us how to protect ourselves from evil people by drawing strength from God. The other Beatitudes (5:7-10) show us how to overcome evil itself. We do so by exercising the virtues of mercy, purity, and peacemaking:

> Blessed are the merciful, for they will be shown mercy. Blessed are the pure in heart, for they will see God. Blessed are the peacemakers, for they will be called children of God. (5:7-10)

In a conflict, we usually think of ourselves as the victim. But the Beatitudes teach us to become a responsible party in the reconciliation process. They force us to shift the focus from feeling sorry for ourselves to thinking about the perpetrator. When we do so, it empowers us to conquer evil.

This contrasts markedly with secular thinking, which tends to place all the responsibility for reconciliation on the offending party. But the teaching that the victim should actively work toward reconciliation is also found in the desert fathers and the Orthodox Churches. Spiritual formation in the Orthodox tradition includes learning to react to an offense with sympathy and prayer.

The Beatitudes and the desert fathers bid us to look within our own hearts when we are in conflict. We cannot bring peace to others unless we first achieve peace within ourselves. Our own pride and anger can exacerbate and prolong a conflict.

On Christmas Eve, 1914, a spontaneous truce broke out between opposing forces in World War I. It began when German soldiers in Belgium began singing Christmas carols and English soldiers responded in kind. Soon, opposing soldiers crossed the battlefield and visited one another. Small gifts like whiskey and chocolate were exchanged and there even were sporting matches. After this, the men were reluctant to go back to war. Enraged politicians and generals forced them to do so. In ensuing years, commanders even ordered artillery bombings on Christmas Eve to prevent peace from breaking out again.

To make peace break out in an organization, we need to have the heart of a peacemaker. Merely following the techniques of conflict management is not enough. We also need to overcome our own pride and destructive anger and to replace it with the spiritual virtues of humility and compassion and non-judgmentalism.

22
Choosing to Forgive

Once when I worked as a gardener, I encountered a weed from hell. It was an ordinary-looking plant but as I began tugging at it, I discovered it had a tap root that raced deep into the soil. Sharp thorns, which easily pierced my thick gloves, covered not only the stalk but the root as well. I dug deeper and deeper and pulled and hacked at it for a whole hour. Once into that fight, I was determined for that blasted root never to grow back.

In the end, the weed won. I yanked out as much as I could without the use of explosives and then simply gave up on a hot summer's day. Yet, I knew it would reach surface again. Bitter roots are like that.

In Jesus' time, the root of bitterness ran deep in many hearts. The Roman army had humiliated Judea for decades. Thousands of Jews lost their lives in periodic attempts at freedom. Yet, Jesus told his followers to "Love your enemies and pray for those who persecute you."

He accepted none of his countrymen's reasons to be bitter. He accepts none of ours. We may think we have a right to be bitter or resentful, but Jesus says it simply is not an option since it can affect our eternal destinies. Instead, we are to overcome bitterness with forgiveness and be like God. "Be perfect, as your heavenly father is perfect," he told us (Matthew 5:48). He also told us to forgive others in our prayers, "if you hold anything against anyone" (Mark 11:25).

Leaders will always find a reason to become bitter. It may be the people who fail us, or those who talk about us. It may be the unfair scrutiny we receive, or the hard work which goes unnoticed. We are responsible for everything, yet not everything is under our control. Through the years, resentment can build up like rust in a pipe.

Yet, we are to avoid becoming bitter.

One way is by practicing unconditional forgiveness — intentionally forgiving others whether or not they admit their fault. The purpose of unconditional forgiveness is to get rid of the toxic waste, whether or not we are proved right. If we wait for people to admit their fault before we forgive them, we're often left to stew in our own juices.

It is to our benefit to forgive unconditionally, since bitter leaders never amount to much. The opportunities they find never equal their talent, nor do they ever thrive like they should. The reason is simple: no one likes to have vinegary people around. When we choose to forgive, we also are choosing a better future for ourselves.

THE EMBATTLED MIDDLE-MANAGER

Middle-management leaders especially have to watch out for bitterness, squeezed as they are between the rank-and-file and senior management. When we field tested this book, a number of leaders said, "We work under a horrible boss. What can a godly leader do?"

Certainly one thing we can do is to maintain our own spiritual authority. Bad bosses are like terrible tykes — they lack the emotional maturity to handle their feelings of power.

The best way to manage people like that is to be mature ourselves. We are not responsible for the dysfunction of others; we are only responsible for our own mental and spiritual health. This means, when dealing with a difficult boss, we should continue to be open and respectful — being pro-active in solving problems, staying on-task and not allowing an issue to become petty and personal. We can give our positive feedback when management acts in a responsible way. Praying for the leaders we serve under also is very important.

The Anglican *Book of Common Prayer* reminds us: "to honor those in authority and to meet their just demands." In other words, sometimes a good leader must also be a good and wise follower of senior leaders.

THE GOAL OF FORGIVENESS

The final goal of forgiveness is always full reconciliation.

I once frequented a blighted neighborhood haunted by fire-gutted buildings. When the buildings were razed, we remembered them every time we passed the empty lots. In time, a new neighborhood was born when beautiful townhouses were built and families moved in and filled the streets with salsa music. It was only after the new neighborhood was built that we finally forgot about the rotted buildings.

The process of reconciliation is like that. Some people never tear down their bitter buildings. They see them every day as they pass by. Others level their buildings, but then they see empty lots for the rest of their lives. Only some of us create a new neighborhood and experience true healing happen.

The ultimate goal of forgiveness is reconciliation — healing the past by finding a future. This can be a messy process. People may have to experience consequences for their actions, even legal consequences, before they will change. But always the goal is the same: to forget the old neighborhood in order to live in the new.

ORGANIZATIONAL FORGIVENESS

Forgiveness is for organizations not just for individuals.

When an organization practices forgiveness, the people within it together choose to leave behind their resentment and grudges over a perceived harm and they work toward a new future. Forgiveness characterizes healthy organizations.

Organizational forgiveness is not an attempt to minimize harm. Instead, it is a response to keep harm from becoming part of the organization's culture. It ends internal dysfunctions by healing bitterness, making peace and creating a positive outcome. It frees people so they can move forward optimistically.

Organizational forgiveness is essential in a downsized organization. Almost always, such organizations fall into conflict, resentment, blame and scapegoating. Attitudes turn rigid, preventing the organization from finding the resiliency it needs to create a new future. To break the downward cycle, people must forgive the harm.

In one hospital I served, a budget crisis threatened jobs. The executive leadership made an extraordinary effort to lay-off as few people as possible by reducing costs. They were honest about the problem and made personal sacrifices themselves. In the end, the staff avoided turning bitter and even were deeply appreciative of what was being done for them. They willingly made their own sacrifices to help.

On the other hand, I served another organization which had downsized due to leadership scandals. The people in it were divided and bitter. My leadership in that institution became a matter of helping people to get over their past. In a series of dicey meetings, we worked through the bitterness and helped people to develop positive attitudes.

Perhaps the most noted example of organizational forgiveness occurred in South Africa after apartheid ended in 1990. For fifty years, the apartheid regime had kept the races apart. Terrible, gruesome killings happened and the minority whites adopted a dehumanizing attitude toward the majority black citizens. Atrocities, such as the Sharpeville massacre of 1960, embittered many. When apartheid ended and the majority races came to power, a bloodbath was expected.

Yet, the national leadership at that time, which included Nelson Mandela and Bishop Desmond Tutu, exemplified forgiveness. Upon his election as president of South Africa, Mandela established the

Truth and Reconciliation Commission, chaired by
Bishop Tutu. It granted complete amnesty to all
apartheid-motivated crimes — including torture,
murder and rape — provided that the confessor
spoke publicly and voluntarily, telling the whole
truth and acknowledging the wrong which had
been done.

The Commission helped to create a new South
Africa. Bishop Tutu remarked, "As I listened to the
stories of victims I marveled at their magnanimity,
that after so much suffering, instead of lusting for
revenge, they had this extraordinary willingness to
forgive."

When we are harmed, we feel we have a right to
be bitter. Usually, forgiveness is the last thing on
our minds. Yet, bitterness makes us unhappy and,
eventually, we just get sick of it all. The way back
to happiness, Jesus teaches, is by forgiving.

Forgiveness can be difficult, since it runs contrary
to our emotions. Yet, once we do it, it frees us
from the harm that happened. Evil does not have to
affect our lives forever. We can find love and God
again.

Epilogue

Aristotle was the first to think that organizations can be virtuous, not just individuals. When an organization is virtuous, it is relatively free from dysfunction and it flourishes with good will and positive energy. It is not just being ethical or dutiful in its operational norms, but also it becomes characterized by high morale, happiness and excellence.

Aristotle used the word *eudaimonia*, "good spirit," to describe this thriving state of being. Today, we talk about a flourishing organization having *synergy*. But organizational virtue is more than people working well together. There also seems to be a stockpile of goodness that just overflows.

Arran Caza, a leading researcher in organizational virtue, describes what happened after three international students had lost everything in a fire. Within days, their school community replaced their lost housing, clothes and computers free of charge. Fellow students also reconstructed missing class notes and donated a generous sum of money to help their classmates. It was an eruption of organizational virtue. [1]

In a similar situation, I witnessed an entire city rally to aid the members of an African-American church whose new sanctuary had been destroyed by arson. People from all walks of life came together to do everything in their power to heal the pain.

This reminds us of the biblical concept of peace. In the Bible, the Hebrew word for peace, *shalom*, means more than a mere absence of war. It is a peace that overflows with the reign of God. Everything wrong has been made right and all people are allowed to flourish and reach their highest potential. Poetically, it is when:

> Love and faithfulness meet together;
> righteousness and peace kiss each other. (Psalm 85:10).

The scriptures describe shalom as marked by justice and reconciliation, when the wolf and the lamb, the calf and the lion all dwell together in unity. Most importantly, it is said to come because of the wise and godly leadership of the Messiah-King. He is the one of whom it is said: "Righteousness will be his belt and faithfulness the sash around his waist," (Isaiah 11:5-7).

---

1 Arran Caza, "Organizational and Leadership Virtues and the Role of Forgiveness" in Journal of Leadership and Organizational Studies, 22 June 2002.

When we lead others in a spiritual way, we are bringing this biblical shalom-peace to our organizations. The ultimate goal of spiritual leadership is to use godly wisdom to make an organization pulse with life.

Currently, I am involved in a city filled with poverty and crime. A group of us recently sponsored a seminar called "Hope in the City." We invited a number of speakers to come who are bringing hope to our troubled city.

One speaker was a nun who maintains a home for women just released from prison. The women have complex personal problems that almost guarantee future jail-time. They lack the basic living skills of self-respect, interpersonal relations and productivity.

When the women first come to the home, they are suspicious and usually say, "No one gives away something for nothing." The reply they are always given is, "You have to learn to soften your heart now." In the home, the women experience safety and love. They learn how to live. After eleven months, they are ready for a try at life again.

Another speaker was a lawyer who bought a home in the city where he houses Christian university interns. They spend a year there, getting jobs in the city and spending the rest of their time in service programs.

A third speaker told how her religious organization allowed the urban poor to farm their land. They are part of an initiative that now involves 100 families, 90 urban youth and a farm store that supplies cheap produce to the city. Bishop Desmond Tutu once said:

> The world is hungry for goodness and it recognizes it when it sees it. There is something in all of us that hungers after the good and true, and when we glimpse it in people, we applaud them for it. We long to be just like them. Their inspiration reminds us of the tenderness for life that we all can feel. [2]

The world is hungering to be led by deep people. We want leaders who will bring biblical shalom-peace into our agencies, organizations, churches, schools and governments. You can be one of those people.

---

2 Kim S. Cameron et al. Positive Organizational Scholarship: Foundations of a New Discipline (Berrett-Koehler, San Francisco, 2003), pg. 60.

Further Reading

While there are hundreds of books available in the fields of spirituality and leadership, the following works are a good place to start and should be readily available through book distributors.

BIBLE READING / THE STORY OF GOD

Bright, John. *The Kingdom of God*

Fee, Gordon D. and Douglas Stuart. *How to Read the Bible for All It's Worth*

COMMUNITY

Bonhoeffer, Dietrich. *Life Together*

LEADERSHIP AND HUMAN BROKENNESS

Johnson, Craig E. *Meeting the Ethical Challenges of Leadership*

McIntosh, Gary L. and Samuel D. Rima, Sr. *Overcoming the Dark Side of Leadership: The Paradox of Personal Dysfunction*

Walker, Simon. *Leading out of Who You Are: Discovering the Secret of Undefended Leadership*

SPIRITUALITY

Calhoun, Adele Ahlberg. *Spiritual Disciplines Handbook*

Foster, Richard J. *Streams of Living Water*

Foster, Richard J. *Celebration of Discipline*

Johnson, Reginald. *Your Personality and the Spiritual Life*

Palmer, G. E. H., Philip Sherrard and Kallistos Ware, trans and eds. *The Philokalia*, Vol 1.

Acknowledgements

This book originally was developed for the seminar, "*Being a Godly Leader*," sponsored by Interserve, an international Christian service organization. Our thanks go to David Allen and Paul Bendor-Samuel for making the seminar possible and for the early seminar presenters — Winnie Thuma, Karen Tan and Harvey Shepard.

Doug Stewart of IFES mentored both of the authors and has their deep respect. Others who provided helpful advice include Hallie and Len Cowen, Susan Currie, Tom Ashbrook and Kit and Tricia McDermott — all spiritual formation leaders.

Dr. Liu Ming of China, a professor of management, adroitly evaluated an early version of the manuscript, as did Bob Morris of Canada, a dedicated international leader. Finally, our gratitude goes to our supportive families.

Dr. David Teague has forty years of experience as a pastoral and mission leader. He lectures occasionally at Gordon-Conwell Theological Seminary and conducts seminars. Dr. Harvey Shepard is a physician serving in Asia.

LaVergne, TN USA
13 August 2010
193247LV00006B/100/P